Attacking Drills

of the
World's Top Teams and Coaches

Edited by
Mike Saif

Published by
WORLD CLASS COACHING

First published April, 2002 by
WORLD CLASS COACHING 9205 W. 131 Terr, Overland Park, KS 66213 (913) 402-0030

ISBN 0-9718218-0-1

Copyright © WORLD CLASS COACHING 2002

The content of this book was originally published as magazines in the USA and UK.

Edited by Mike Saif

WORLD CLASS COACHING would like to thank worldofsoccer.com for the use of the graphics

Published by

WORLD CLASS COACHING

Table of Contents

Attacking Drills

of the
World's Top Teams and Coaches

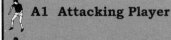

IK Start ll Norway

Contributed by subscriber, Phil Barber. Phil observed the following practice of the I.K... Start ll youth team who plays in the Norwegian First Division. Phil was invited to progress the session, which he did with the practice in diagram 3. While the practices are very simple, they are extremely effective and were practiced at game speed and for over 30 minutes. Phil noted that the players had an extremely businesslike and enthusiastic attitude during practice.

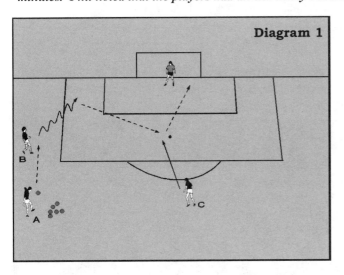

Finishing From Cut-Backs

A passes to B.

- B dribbles inside the penalty area toward the end-line and cuts the ball back toward the penalty spot.
- C finishes with a side-foot shot in the corner of the goal.
- Have three or four players in each position.

Coaching Points

- Quality passes from A and B
- B should have his head up so he can see C's position
- Quality of shot from C - he should 'pass' the ball into the corner of the goal
- C should be aware of the position of the goalkeeper

Finishing From a Lay-Off

A plays a lofted pass to B.
B lays the ball into the path of incoming C.
C finishes with a side-foot shot into the corner of the goal.

Coaching Points

- Quality of the lofted pass is critical
- The lay-off should be into the path of incoming C so that he can shoot the ball without breaking his stride
- C should adjust his body shape depending on the lay-off

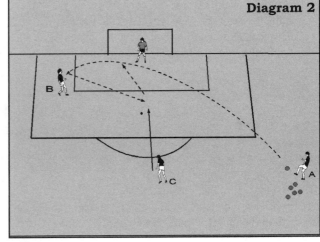

Progression

A feeds the ball through the legs of B to C.
C plays a cross-field pass to D. C and B then advance on goal.
D lays the ball off to E.
E passes one touch to running F.
F delivers a cross or a pull-back to B or C who finishes on goal.

Coaching Points

- All previous coaching points
- It may be necessary for B and C to lay the ball off for each other in order to create a good shooting opportunity
- Quality of passes, crosses and lay-offs are of paramount importance to the practice

Columbus Crew

Contributed by Greg Andrulis.

Warm-Up

The players start most practices with a variation of 5 v 2 or 6 v 2 in small grids. They are then organized into two teams and each team is split into two groups of four players and positioned in lines as shown in diagram 4. The players perform a variety of passing and movement exercises. After each sequence the players stretch.

The players in line 1 and 2 are one team and lines 3 and 4 are another team. Once the players are warmed up, competition is introduced. For example, the first team to have all their players complete passes and end up in their original starting positions win. Or the first team to complete 20 consecutive passes wins.

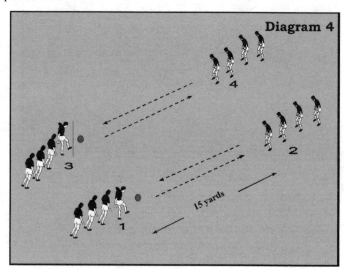

Variations

- Players in opposite lines dribble toward each other and do a takeover
- Using two touches, the players pass the ball to the opposite line and follow their pass joining the back of the opposite line. The players' first touch should be at an angle to create movement and a passing lane
- Use two touches as before but vary the technique with just the inside of the foot, outside of the foot, etc.
- Use two touches, pass the ball to the opposite line and backpedal to join the back of your own line

Progression

The first player in line 1 passes to line 3.
The first player in line 3 passes to line 4.
The first player in line 4 passes to line 2.
The first player in line 2 passes to line 1.
After passing, the players follow their pass and join the end of the line they have passed to. The sequence continues with the next player in line 1 passing to line 3.

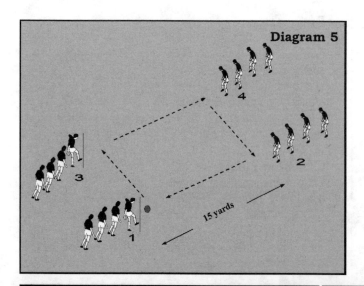

Progressions

- Change directions
- Once the exercise is flowing, a second ball is introduced starting at line 4.

Coaching Points

- Weight of the pass
- Direction of the passes
- Control the ball across the body
- Play to feet

Columbus Crew

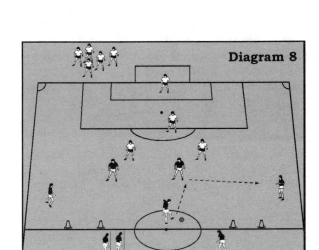

Diagram 6

Half-Field Competition

The two teams now compete in a variety of exercises to goal. One team is attacking and one team is defending. The ball is in play until a goal is scored, a goal-kick or throw-in is given, or if the defending team scores a goal through the small goals (cones) on the half-line. This encourages second chances and transition. After 10 attacks, the teams change roles. Keep track of the score to make the game competitive.

Sequence One

3 v 2 to goal with a goalkeeper.

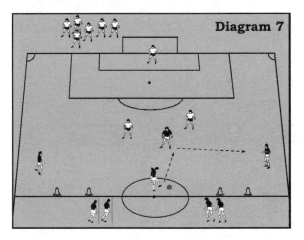

Diagram 7

Sequence Two

4 v 2 to goal with a goalkeeper

Sequence Three

5 v 3 to goal with a goalkeeper

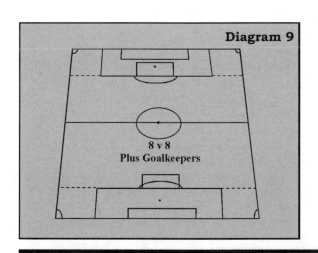

Diagram 8

Diagram 9

8 v 8
Plus Goalkeepers

9 v 9 Game

Practice ended with a game on a full field with the goals positioned on the top of each penalty area. Full size goals and goalkeepers are used.

The winner of the game was the first team to three goals or a maximum of six minutes, whichever comes first. In this game, the six minutes came first so the game was decided by an MLS shoot-out.

Manchester United U19's

In February 1999 I was fortunate enough to spend a day with David Williams, youth team coach at Manchester United. As usual, it was a pleasure to observe Williams work with his players. On this day, the players trained in the morning and afternoon. The morning was a passing and possession session. The afternoon session (below) was spent working on shooting and finishing. When the players practice twice a day, the morning session usually consists of some form of a small-sided game and the afternoon session is usually spent working on technique.

Warm-Up

The players organized themselves in pairs. Each pair juggled a ball between them and did the following sequence.

• Juggle and hit the ball 25 feet in the air and then head it to his partner
• Juggle and hit the ball 25 feet in the air for his partner to head and continue juggling
• Juggle and hit the ball 25 feet in the air for his partner to control with his thigh and continue juggling
• Juggle and hit the ball 25 feet in the air for his partner to control with the inside of his foot and continue juggling
• Juggle and hit the ball 25 feet in the air for his partner to control with his chest and continue juggling

Coaching Point

Adjust body position to get in line with the ball

Shooting

On half-field with two full size goals and goalkeepers, the players are organized in lines at each side of the goals. The coach is positioned in the center of the field. The first player in line 1 passes the ball to the coach. He and the first player in line 2 both run on opposite sides of the coach. The coach lays off a pass for one of the players to shoot one touch. Both players follow the shot for any rebounds then join the back of lines 3 and 4. The drill continues with the front players in lines 3 and 4 going in the opposite direction.

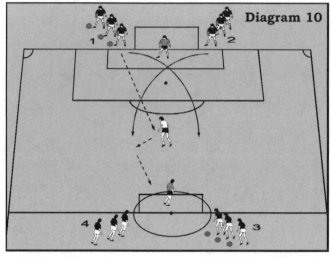

Coaching Points

• The coach lays the ball off to either player randomly so the players don't know who is going to shoot
• The coach varies the type of lay-off

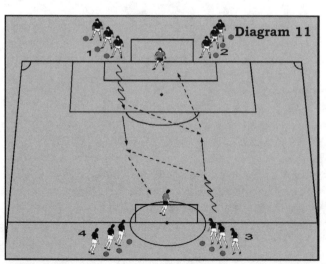

Shooting

The first players in lines 1 and 3 dribble toward each other, pass the ball across the field to each other and then hit one touch shots. (Two touches were taken if needed.) Player 1 joins the back of line 4 and player 3 joins the back of line 2 so their next attempt will be with their opposite foot. Then the first players in lines 2 and 4 dribble toward each other and continue the drill.

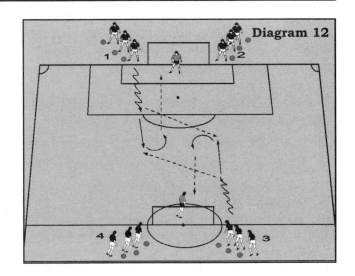

Diagram 12

Progression

This time, when the players receive the pass, they turn and shoot on their own goal.

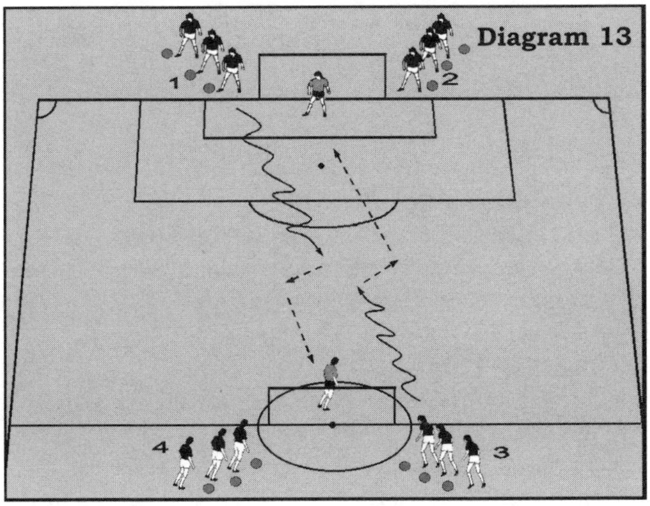

Diagram 13

Progression

The front players in lines 1 and 3 dribble toward each other, fake to the right of each other and shoot. As before, player 1 joins the back of line 4 and player 3 joins the back line 2 so that they use their opposite foot on their next turn.

Practice ended with an 11 v 11 one-touch game on half-field with lines extending from the edge of the penalty area as was used in the morning session. If the ball went out-of-bounds, it was started with a kick-in. If a shot went wide or above the goal, the shooting player had to retrieve the ball while the game continued with another ball, and his team played one player short until he got back.

Women's World Cup Team

Contributed by Jay Hoffman, assistant coach, U.S. Women's National Team. Prior to each session the players begin to warm up on their own with running and stretching. This usually lasts for about 10 minutes. Running includes different variations of forward, sideways and backwards combinations of jogging to eventually sprinting, jumping, skipping, etc. This is designed to increase the heart rate and prepare for the upcoming training session.

Warm-Up With the Ball
Players (already divided into their teams) in partners, in a confined area play pass, receive and move.

Coaching Points
- Accurate passes - weight, type, to feet or space, preparation of the ball to pass
- Receiving on the move, first touch in preparation to play the ball quickly, correct body surface to receive the ball, balance
- Tactical running after the pass, changing of speed and direction as if to get behind a defender
- Tactical running by the receiving player, timing to be able to sprint for the ball into space or checking for the ball based upon the passing player preparing to pass

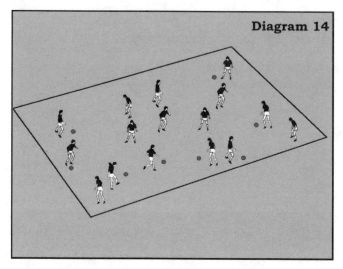

Diagram 14

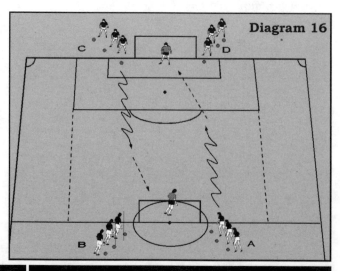

Diagram 15

8 v 8

Technique Under Pressure
Teams divided from the first exercise play 8 v 8 in a confined area (penalty box for example). Players must use at least two touches before they can pass.

Coaching Points
- Tactical implication of technique given the demands of the game
- Technical aspects to maintain possession of the ball as individuals and as a team
- Tactical aspects, team shape, timing of runs, roles of players, principals of play to maintain possession

Finishing - Technical
Using half a field, set up a goal on the half-line and extend the lines from the edge of the penalty area to make an area 44 yards wide.
Players from lines A and C dribble towards goal and shoot. C joins the back of line B and A joins the back of line D. The front players from lines B and D then dribble and shoot. Therefore, all players get to practice shooting with both feet.

Coaching Points
- Weight transfer through the ball
- Body position to shoot the ball, compact, ankle locked, knee over the ball, balance, preparation of the ball to finish.

Diagram 16

C   D

B   A

Women's World Cup Team

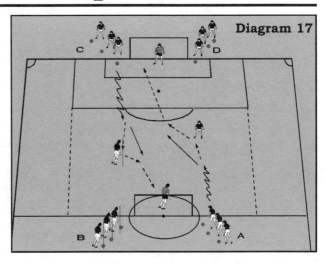

Diagram 17

Variations

- Shooting off the dribble
- Shooting first touch off a through pass
- Shooting off a give-and-go (diagram 17)
- Shooting under pressure - add a defender to the shooter who chases to make the shooter work quickly for all the variations

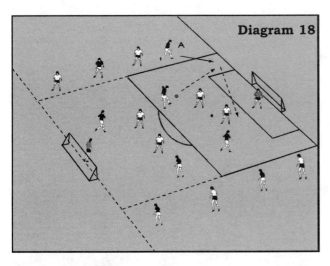

Diagram 18

Finishing Game

Mark out a second 18 x 44-yard area adjoining the penalty area. Two teams play 8 v 8 with full size goals and goalkeepers. Play 4 v 4 on the field with the other four players from each team positioned on the sidelines as shown in diagram 18. The sideline players cannot score, are limited to one touch and cannot defend against either the opposition's field or sideline players. The sideline players at the respective attacking ends can make runs to the end-line, as player A is doing, to receive a pass (as a player would when getting behind the defense) but he must return to the sideline straight away. Play two minute games then change positions.

Coaching Points

- Technical aspects of finishing
- Tactical aspects of finishing, choice of surface to finish, selection of power v passing to finish, first touch shot v preparation to finish, deception and creating opportunities to finish

Functional Finishing Game

Organize the players as they play in the game (position and system) in the attacking third to half of the field. This aspect varies as to the overall theme of the training for finishing. Play depending on your system and number of players (6 v 4, 7 v 4, 7 v 5) at both ends or a variation at the opposite end. The players only play in their respective halves of the field and the defenders must play the ball out to the attackers so the game flows.

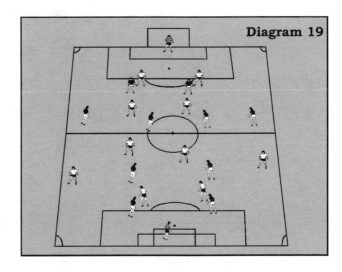

Diagram 19

Variations

Allow players from the back to go forward, limiting the number of touches, and opening the game to play both ways.

Coaching Points

- Technical aspects of playing and finishing
- Tactical aspects of playing and finishing
- Technical and tactical functions of the specific positions

Venice - Serie 'A'

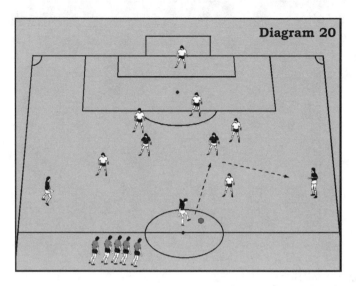

Diagram 20

Half-Field Game

The teams played 5 v 5 on half a field in an attack v defending situation with one team resting. The teams rotated every 2 - 3 minutes.

The coach constantly stopped the game to get across his coaching points. After 15 minutes the game progressed to 8 v 8 with all the players involved and fewer stoppages from the coach.

Coaching Points
- Switching the point of attack
- Overlaps
- Creating shooting opportunities and having the mind-set to shoot whenever possible
- Getting players behind the defense
- Getting the ball wide for crosses

Shooting and Finishing

The goalkeeper starts with the ball. Two players (A and B) are positioned 25 yards from the goal in line with the goalposts. The goalkeeper plays the ball to player A or B (player A in this example) and moves to get the one-touch return.
At the same time, player B chases the goalkeeper to put pressure on him.
The goalkeeper then plays a long pass to a player waiting on the half-line who begins to attack the goal.

Coaching Point
Good clearance/pass from the goalkeeper.

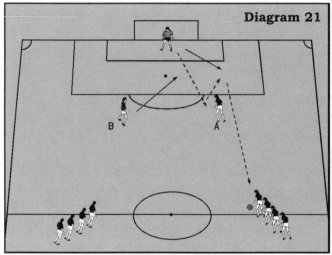

Diagram 21

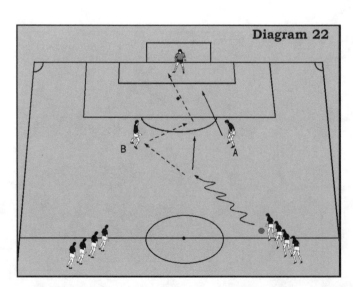

Diagram 22

Following the pass, the goalkeeper quickly retreats back to his goal.
Once the player on the half-line receives the ball, he attacks the goal, plays a give-and-go with player A or B (in this example, player B) and shoots on goal.
Player A reacts to the shot and follows in for any rebounds.
The shooting player then replaces player A.
The goalkeeper and shooter alternate their passes between player A and B.

Coaching Points
- Shots must be on target
- Use both right and left feet to shoot depending on whether player A or B is used for the give-and-go

Chelsea F.C.

Observed at the training ground of English Premier League team, Chelsea Football Club.

Warm-Up

The players came out of the locker room and got themselves into pairs or small groups and practiced juggling or passing and moving. It took about 15 minutes before all the players and coaches were on the field and ready to start. The team warm-up was a 10-minute run followed by stretches. This was followed by 10 minutes of fast footwork drills..

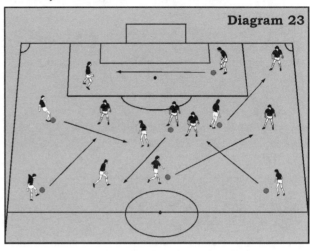

Diagram 23

The players were then organized into pairs and worked on a half-field passing and moving about 25 yards apart doing the following combinations:

- Firm, driven passes followed by a shout of "hold" or "turn" for the partner to react accordingly
- Pass to partner then follow for a give-and-go
- Pass to partner then follow for a return pass into space

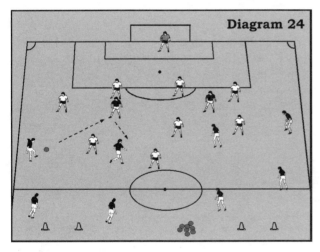

Diagram 24

Attack v Defense

On the same half-field, place two small goals about 3 yards apart 15 yards past the half-line. The attacking team is made up of a full team of 10 players organized in a 4-4-2 formation. The defending team is comprised of a goalkeeper and eight field players consisting of four defenders and four midfielders. The attacking team attempts to score on the full size goal and the defending team attempts to score in either of the small goals. The game lasted for 15 minutes with the coach focusing on coaching the defenders.

Coaching Points - Defenders

- Push out after a clearance (offside was in effect)
- Force the play in one direction
- When in possession, get the ball wide, early

Crossing and Finishing

On the same half-field, the players are organized as shown in diagram 25.
Player A runs and turns to receive a pass from player B, passes back to player B with one touch and continues his run to the edge of the penalty area.
Player B passes wide to the first player in line C.
Player C runs toward the corner and crosses for incoming players D and E who attempt to finish with one touch, or one player can set the other player with a one-touch lay-off.
The next players in line continue the drill by passing to the opposite flank.

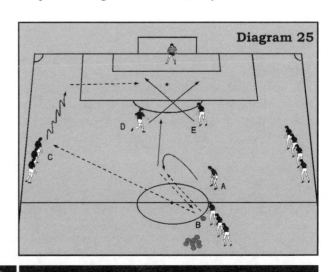

Diagram 25

Chelsea F.C.

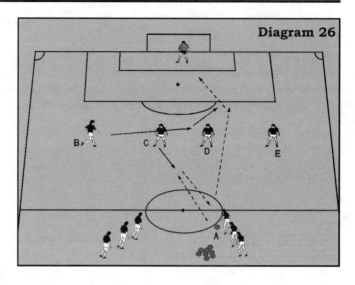

Diagram 26

Finishing by Beating the Offside Trap

Line four players across the field about 35 yards from goal as shown in diagram 26.

Player A passes to incoming player C.

Player C passes back with one touch to player A.

As this is going on, player B makes a flat run across the field.

Player A passes through the gap of players D and E.

As soon as player A passes the ball, player B breaks to receive the pass in space and finishes on goal.

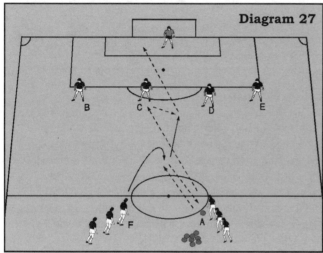

Diagram 27

Shooting

Player A passes to player F.

Player F passes back to player A with one touch and continues his run toward the goal.

Player A passes to player C.

Player C lays off for incoming player F to shoot with one touch.

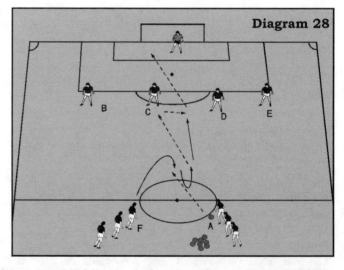

Diagram 28

Variation

The same organization as in diagram 27. This time, player F turns with the ball and passes to player C. Player C lays off with one touch for incoming player F to finish.

Many variations of the shooting drills were done involving players B and E following in for rebounds and players A and F passing to different players. At the end of practice a group of players stayed behind and practiced shooting and crossing.

Brazilian Youth Practices

Submitted by Vinicius Dos Santos. The following practices were observed at the Clube Pequeninos Do Jockey, São Paulo, Brazil in the summer of 1998. Clube Pequeninos Do Jockey is a major youth soccer development program similar to the Tahuichi program in Bolivia. Pequeninos has relationships with many Brazilian, South American and even European Clubs. Their main function is to search and develop new talent for its clubs. Many professional players started their careers at Pequeninos including Ze Roberto of Bayer Leverkussen and the Brazilian National Team. Pequeninos is basically an inner city program. They have around 2,000 players aged 5 - 20 and almost 100 coaches. The following practices for midfield and forward runs were done with the U14 age group.

The session starts with a Brazilian style warm-up, without the ball, comprising of body coordination movements. This is followed by 15 minutes of technical warm-up with the players in pairs using one ball and practicing various techniques. The main part of the session consists of practicing attacking combinations using midfielder and forward runs. These are practiced for 45 minutes starting initially unopposed and gradually adding defenders to make the practice more game realistic. As is the case in most Brazilian training sessions, the practice ends with an 11 v 11 game where the players look to put into effect the combinations they have just practiced.

Attacking Combination One

The center midfielder dribbles the ball toward the left forward. The left forward moves toward the center midfielder and 'shows' for the ball. The right forward moves into the space left by the left forward. The center midfielder plays a give-and-go with the left forward, then passes the ball to the left flank for the running left defender. The left defender has three options:

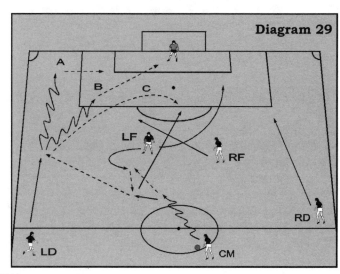

Diagram 29

A. Attack the end-line and cross
B. Diagonal penetration followed by a shot or cross
C. Early cross

Following his pass, the center midfielder runs to the edge of the penalty area looking for any rebounds. The left forward runs to the far post area and the right forward attacks the near post area. Also, the right defender makes a late run into the penalty area.

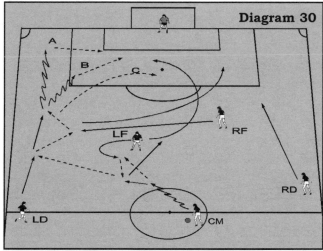

Diagram 30

Attacking Combination Two

Similar to the previous combination, however, this time the right forward moves into the space left by the left forward and continues toward the left flank to play a give-and-go with left defender. For this pattern, the runs into the penalty area are reversed by the left and right forward. When the right forward moves to the left flank for the give-and-go with the left defender, this is the signal for the left forward to make a near post run. The right forward then runs to the far post.

Attacking Combination Three

Diagram 31 is a variation of diagram 30. This time, when the right forward receives the pass from the left defender, he turns and attacks the penalty area giving him three options:

A. Pass toward the end-line for the overlapping left defender
B. Shoot on goal
C. Cross for the left forward to shoot

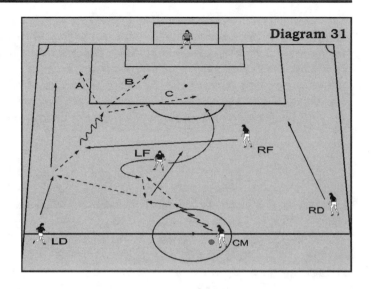

Attacking Combination Four

In this example, the right forward makes his run into the space left by the left forward and then continues toward the left corner end-line. The left defender passes the ball down the line for the running right forward who crosses into the penalty area. The left forward makes a near post run, the center midfielder makes a far post run and the left defender runs to the edge of the penalty area.

Attacking Combination Five

Diagram 33 is a variation of diagram 32. This time, when the right forward receives the pass from the left defender, he cuts the pass back to the left defender.

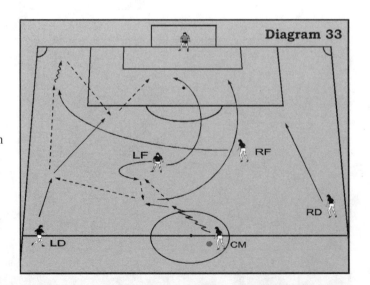

Attacking in the Final Third

This session was part of the Coaches' Super Clinic conducted by Reedswain in New Jersey, February 3, 4 and 5. Conducted by Lauren Gregg, the assistant coach for the U.S. Women's National Team that won the 1999 World Cup, the session was done indoors in a 40 x 20-yard area. When practicing outdoors, a larger area would be used.

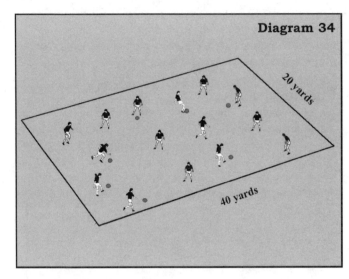

Diagram 34

Warm-Up

In a 40 x 20-yard area, organize 15 players with seven balls and pass and move.

Coaching Points

- Control your receiving touch away from an imaginary defender
- Pass with the outside or inside of foot and try to bend the ball
- Change of pace after your pass

Diagram 35

Warm-Up

Organize the players in groups of three with the two outside players 40 yards apart and one player in the middle as shown in diagram 35.

Player A passes to player B.

Player B passes with one touch back to player A.

Player A attempts to bend the pass around player B to player C at the other end.

Player A then moves into the middle to receive the pass from player C and player B takes player A's position.

Coaching Points

- One touch passes if possible
- Practice with the inside and outside of both feet

Overlap Combination One

Player A passes to player B then overlaps player B.

Player B passes to incoming player C then makes a far post run.

Player C receives the ball, turns and passes to overlapping player A then makes a near post run.

Player A crosses to the near or far post for players B and C.

Coaching Points

- The first player into the goalbox should make the near post run
- Player A should look and see his options before deciding where to cross the ball

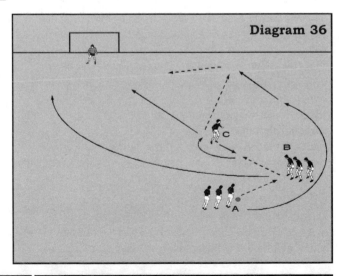

Diagram 36

Attacking in the Final Third

Diagram 37

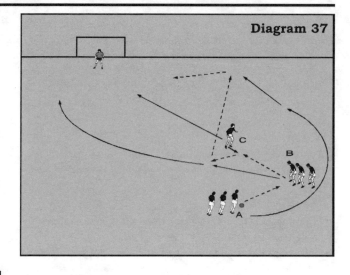

Overlap Combination Two

Use the same organization as in the previous exercise, however, this time player B plays a give-and-go with player C and passes to overlapping player A.

Coaching Point

Player C would still make his run to the near post as he would arrive in the goalbox first.

Diagram 38

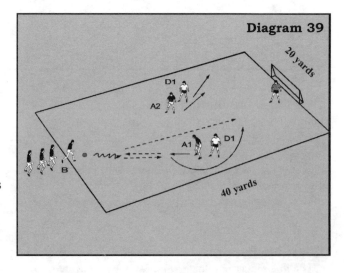

Progression

Progress the exercise by adding a defender as shown in diagram 38. The defender has two choices:

* To defend player B or C before they make the pass to overlapping player A
* Cover player A forcing player B or C to dribble inside with the ball

Let the players 'play'. For the exercise to work well, the attacking players should be allowed to use any combinations depending on the option that the defender chooses and who the unmarked player is.

Two v Two

Organize two forwards, A1 and A2 and two defenders, D1 and D2 in a 20 x 40-yard area with one goal and a goalkeeper.

The first player in line, player B, dribbles the ball in and passes to the forward who comes and 'shows' for the ball (player A1).

Player B passes to player A1 who passes straight back. Following his pass, player A1 spins and runs around the outside of player D1.

Player B plays a pass into the path of player A1 who attempts a one-touch finish.

Again, let the players 'play'. If the defender follows the run of player A1, then player B should attack the space and shoot.

Diagram 39

20 yards

40 yards

Coaching Points

* As one forward checks toward the ball the other forward should move away to create space for the pass from player B
* The quality of the final pass from player B is critical

Attacking in the Final Third

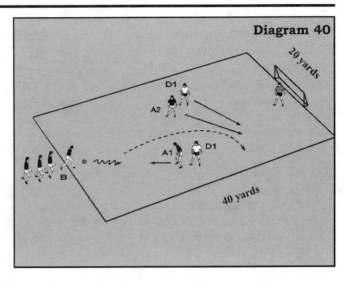

Two v Two Progression

As player A1 checks toward the ball, player A2 runs into the space created by player A1.

Player B plays a pass over the head of players A1 and D1. Player A2 attempts a one-touch finish.

Coaching Points

- The two forwards, players A1 and A2, need to communicate and learn to read each other's movements - eye contact and definite movement helps
- Again, the quality of the pass from player B is critical

Five v Three

Organize three defenders and five forwards attacking a goal as shown in diagram 41. The objective is for the attacking team to move the ball from one flank to the other looking for shooting opportunities. Balls can be passed into the forward's feet for them to lay off for shots or they can turn and attempt to shoot themselves.

Coaching Point

Player A can look to reproduce the previously practiced overlap situations.

Small-Sided Game

This small-sided game is usually played in an area the size of two 18-yard penalty areas. Organize two teams of three players plus goalkeepers. Position four neutral players at the sides of the goals. Play 3 v 3. The player in possession can pass to a perimeter player who passes back into play with one touch to the passer or one of his teammates as shown in diagram 42.

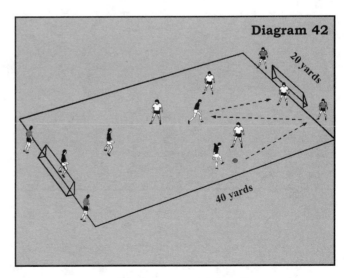

Editors Note...Lauren conducted a very lively session in a small area. Again, it must be emphasized that when conducting these exercises outdoors, larger areas would be used.

Kansas City Wizards

A finishing session contributed by then assistant coach of the Kansas City Wizards, Ken Fogarty.

Warm-Up
Organize four groups around the penalty area as shown in diagram 43. Do the following five variations for 2-3 minutes each with two minutes of stretching in between. The explanations are for the A and B groups, however, the C and D groups go at the same time. Following each pass or shot, the players jog to the back of the opposite line doing various techniques such as, high knees, long strides, high heels behind, etc.

- A passes to B who side foots a pass to the near post for the goalkeeper to collect.
- The groups on the edge of the penalty area move closer in line with the penalty spot. A serves the ball from his hands for B to side foot a volley to the near post for the goalkeeper to collect.
- Repeat the side foot volleys from the edge of the penalty area.
- The groups on the edge of the penalty area move closer again in line with the penalty spot. Player A serves the ball from his hands for B to head to the near post for the goalkeeper to collect.
- For the final variation, the players move back to the edge of the penalty area. Player A passes to B who shoots and attempts to score. This time the goalkeepers alternate to save the shots and the players sprint to the opposite line.

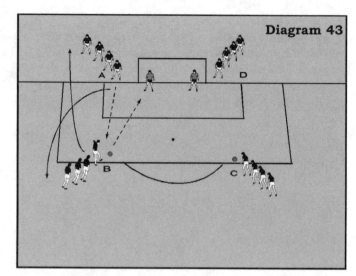

Diagram 43

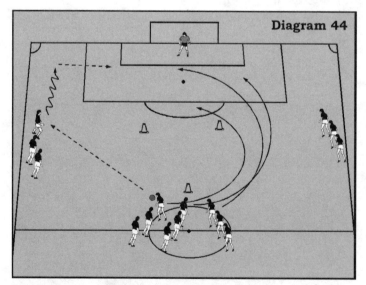

Diagram 44

Crossing and Finishing
Organize the players in groups of three as shown in diagram 44 and rotate positions frequently. The ball is passed to either flank and the three players then run around the opposite cone. For instance, in diagram 44, the ball is served to the left flank and the three players then run around the right cone. The flank player attacks the end line and crosses for the incoming three runners.

Coaching Points
- The flank players should cross in one or two touches
- The three running players must divide the runs to the near post, far post and the edge of the penalty area
- The first person round the cone should run to the near post

Kansas City Wizards

Competitive Finishing

Using the same set up as in diagram 44, organize the players into two teams with players from both teams at each position. Remove the cones. Each team takes turns passing to one of their flank players and then the three players make their runs into the penalty area. The first team to score 10 goals wins.

Coaching Points

• As in diagram 29
• Finish with one touch if possible
• Quality crosses
• Accuracy over power

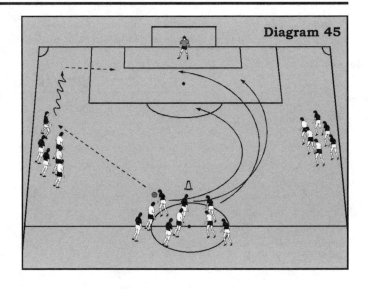

Diagram 45

Diagram 46

20 yards

30 yards

Small-Sided Game

Organize the players into three teams of six and play 6 v 6 with goalkeepers and full-sized goals on a 20 x 30-yard field. The third team rests. The coach is on the perimeter of the field with a supply of balls and starts the game by serving a ball into the middle of the field. As balls go out-of-bounds, the coach continues to serve balls in to keep the game flowing. The first team to score three goals wins and the losing team is replaced by the third team waiting on the sidelines.

Coaching Points

• Quick decision making and finishing
• Accuracy over power
• Look for rebounds defensively and offensively

End practice with a cool down of jogging and stretching.

Contributed by Dave Clarke, Coach, Windsor World Class - Snickers Under 16 Girls National Champions; Head Women's Soccer Coach - Quinnipiac University; Coordinator, Connecticut Coaching License Program.

Windsor World Class U16 Girls

Windsor World Class Soccer Club was formed by National Staff Coach, Tom Goodman in 1987 and is located in Windsor, Connecticut. The club has 10 teams playing at the premier level in Connecticut and all of them train and play at Northwest Park in Windsor.

The current Under 17 team has been playing together since Under 12 and they won the club's first National Championship in Orlando last summer. 1999 was my first year coaching the team, but I had previously coached many of the players with the Connecticut ODP. All but two of the players have represented Connecticut at the ODP level. Five have been in the regional pool and two are current members of the Under 17 National Team.

The team had a disappointing season in 1998 and the players were focused on and committed to re-establishing the team at the premier level in 1999. Besides winning the National Title, the team also won the Region One championship, CJSA Open Cup, CJSA Premier League, Massapequa Tournament and the Nordic Tournament. So far in 2000 the team has won the Jefferson Cup in Virginia.

The focus of the team to date has not been to repeat as national champions. The only goal is to make the Connecticut Open Cup final and hopefully progress to Regionals again. The players and staff are more focused on the players improving and playing attractive soccer than on retaining their national title.

We have 17 players on our roster for the 2000 season and all of the players were at this practice session. All year our practice sessions have focused on passing and possession and this is one of our final practices before State Cup play begins on May 7. The session lasted for two hours.

Warm-Up: 15-20 Minutes

The players jog around the park where we train for 5-10 minutes. They jog in a group and can stop, stretch and talk, but MUST be ready to play/train when they come back to the field. During this time the players are free to talk and socialize. It is an important part of the session as it allows team mates to become "friends" which in turn improves team chemistry.

Then, organize into groups with players in each group 10 yards apart, with one ball per group. Pass to the first player in the opposite group then jog to the end of the opposite group. Players can play one or two touch, but must concentrate on pace and proper technique.

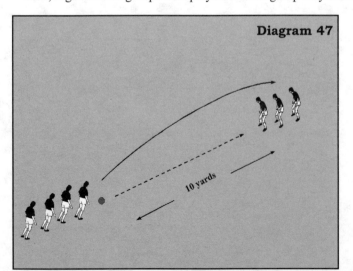

Diagram 47

10 yards

Progression

- After the pass, jog to the end of the opposite group with heels up, knees up, skipping, etc.
- After the pass, players must sprint to the end of the opposite group
- Emphasis on talking and demanding the ball - the receiving players must say the passer's name before receiving the ball
- Players should follow the pass as quickly as possible and try to beat the ball there
- Emphasis on quality passing

Conditioning: 20-25 Minutes

We have been training outside for over two months and have built up a good level of fitness with another five weeks of solid work still to be done. At the present time we are sprinting approximately 1500 yards every practice session. Most of this running is done with the ball or is included in a game when possible.

Organize the players into three groups of five with each group in a 10 x 10 grid as shown. The emphasis here is on the sprint work, but because the ball is used, it also helps the players work on their passing technique and ball control.

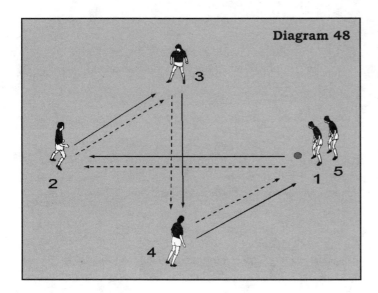

Diagram 48

The two goalkeepers are not included in the sprint work. They work together on goal kicks, crosses, abdominal work, etc.

Sprint Set One

1 passes to 2 and sprints after the pass. 2 passes to 3 and sprints after the pass. 3 passes to 4 and sprints after the pass. 4 passes to 5 and sprints after the pass and 5 passes to 1 and sprints after the pass. Players must run past the player they are passing to. Each player sprints 10 times around the grid for a total of 300 yards.

Players must play two-touch on every execution. They must stop the ball before passing it to the next player, then sprint after the pass trying to beat their pass to the player.

Sprint Set Two

The same as Set One, but the ball must now be played with one touch. A supply of balls is kept beside each group so that the exercise does not have to stop for an errant pass. Emphasis again is on sprinting and working hard, but the players must also concentrate on quality passes.

Sprint Set Three

Each player has a ball. They sprint in the same sequence as Sets One and Two. This time they must run with the ball to the next player in sequence. The next player in sequence runs once the player reaches them.

Sprint Set One was repeated twice, so players did four sets of 300 yards for a total of 1200 yards of sprint work. One minute rest between sets.

In and Out Game: 20-25 Minutes

On a field 36 x 30 yards, play two teams of eight plus a neutral player, each with a keeper in goal, five field players and two support players, one on either side of their own goal. The players have unlimited touches but goals can only be scored by using one touch. This restriction forces defenders to close down quickly, forwards to think and finish quickly and teammates to support the ball quickly. Due to the restriction of space and time in which to play, the pace of this game is very fast and players are forced to play, move and think quickly.

Players on the end line can enter the field when they receive the ball from a teammate. Their nearest teammate must then step off the field. They can also enter the field when a goal is scored or the keepers get possession of the ball in their hands. The team in possession should use their support players as often and as quickly as possible. Each game is played to five goals with the losing team doing 10 tuck jumps each.

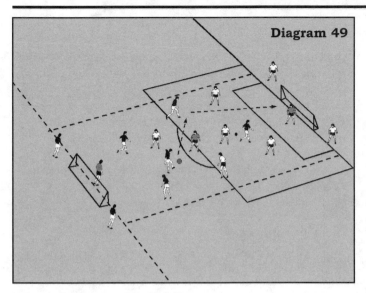

Diagram 49

Coaching Points
- Emphasis on playing one and two touch, playing the way you are facing and looking for the simplest option possible
- Looking for good passing and support
- Awareness of players off the field as to when they can come in and play
- Keepers getting the ball back into play as quickly as possible
- Attitude of defenders to close down quickly
- Attitude of attacking team to finish quickly and accurately

Tactical Game: 35-40 Minutes
The field is set up as shown in diagram 50 with a supply of balls next to each goal. Organize two teams of eight with one neutral player who plays for the team in possession making the game 9 v 8. In this practice, a midfield player was always used as the neutral player. The starting forwards and midfield players were placed on the same team to get them to learn how to work together.

Set Up
For the first five minutes the game is free play to the goals so that the players get used to the dimensions of the field. Keepers must be on their goal line when the opposition has the ball. They can come off their line to support their defenders when their team is in possession.
Offside is in effect in the two 18-yard zones, so the players must time their runs to get in there.
Look for the team in possession of the ball to get players in behind the opposition's defense to create scoring opportunities. The attacking player who receives the ball behind the back four must attack the keeper 1 v 1 and look to score.
If the attacking team scores, they maintain possession and start with the ball from their keeper. If the forward misses or the keeper saves the ball, the defending team now becomes the attacking team and starts with a pass from their keeper.
Only players from the attacking team are allowed in either zone. They can drop in to receive the ball from their keeper or can use their keeper to maintain possession.

Coaching Points
- Emphasis on quality passing, movement on and off the ball, forward runs, and forward passes behind defenders
- Forwards must show for the ball to drag out the defenders and open up space for runners to get in behind the defense
- Look for wide players and overlapping defenders to make runs in behind the defense
- Look for quality support around the ball
- Understanding that the ball must be played into the zone before a run is made
- Attitude of attackers to finish when they are through one-on-one with the keeper
- Keepers should distribute the ball as quickly as possible - this will set up the counter attack as the opposition is now three players down (two attackers plus the neutral player)

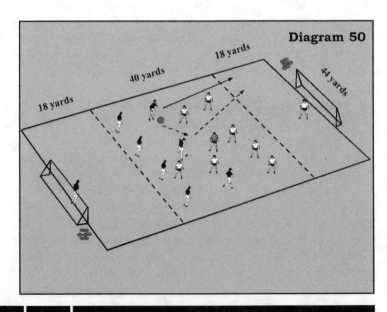

Diagram 50

18 yards

40 yards

18 yards

44 yards

Progression

Allow a second attacker into the zone to support the first attacker. This player is looking for rebounds, crosses pulled back, or a square pass and finish.

Allow one defender to enter the zone to put pressure on either attacker making a 2 v 2 situation and more realistic to the game.

Finish by taking off the restrictions and playing a game, but keep offside in effect. This keeps the spacing and the game as realistic as possible.

Keep score and losing team does 5 extra hills at the end of practice.

Additional Fitness Work: 15-20 minutes

Players finished the session by doing 20 hills next to the field. Players who have missed practice stay and do an additional 20 hills for each practice missed. Each hill is 20 yards for a total of 400 yards sprinted making the total for the session 1600 yards.

Cool Down

Players jog and stretch for five minutes before picking up all the equipment.

Additional Comments

The players worked extremely hard in this session which was one of their best this season. No player enjoys doing fitness work, but my players appreciate doing their work with the ball. The fact that they were so successful in 1999 means they understand the rewards of working hard in practice. Their favorite activity is the 'In and Out' game because it is played in and around the penalty area, has plenty of goals and goalscoring opportunities and they know I rarely stop play in this game.

Chelsea Youth Team

Observed during the regular season, October, 1999.

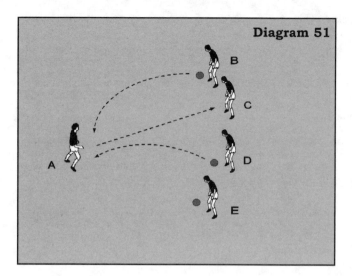

Diagram 51

Warm-Up

After 15 minutes of jogging and stretching, the players split into groups of five as shown. Player A is five yards away from B, C, D and E. Players B, C, D and E have three balls between them. They take turns passing the ball from their hands to A who volleys back with either foot to the player without the ball.

Player A is constantly on his toes and players B, C, D and E pass the ball quickly to keep A moving. Progress to chest-volley, head-volley, etc. Rotate positions every minute.

Timing Offensive Runs

Organize the players on a half field as shown. Player A1 passes to A3 then starts his run across the field. A3 passes the ball down the center of the field to A1. As soon as A3 passes, A1 breaks his run to go forward and runs onto the pass to shoot on goal. A3 takes A1's position and A1 joins the back of A4's line.
The exercise continues with A2 passing to A4.

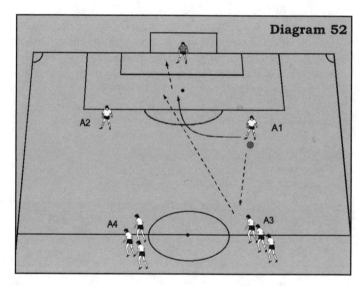

Diagram 52

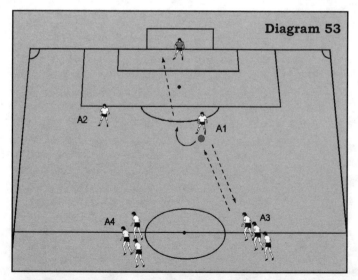

Diagram 53

Turning and Shooting

The same set up as in the previous exercise but this time player A1 starts in the center of the field, passes to A3, receives the return pass, turns and shoots. In this exercise the coach acted as a passive defender.

Chelsea Youth Team

Diagram 54

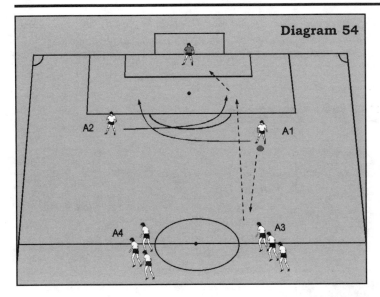

Progression

Continue with the same set up as diagram 53.
When A1 passes to A3, both A1 and A2 make runs across the field.
A3 passes the ball to either A1 or A2 to shoot.
A1 and A2 time their runs so that they break toward goal as soon as A3 passes to them.

Diagram 55

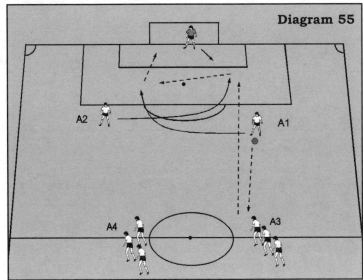

Progression

If the goalkeeper comes out and makes the shot difficult, A2 has the option of pulling the ball back across the goalbox for A1 to shoot.

Diagram 56

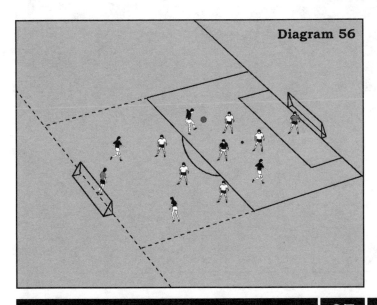

Small-Sided Game

Practice ended with a 5 v 5 small-sided game in an area the size of two penalty areas with full size goals and goalkeepers as shown. The emphasis of the game was to take quick, early shooting opportunities

Dick Bate

This session was conducted by Dick Bate at the Coaches' Super Clinic conducted by Reedswain in New Jersey, February 3, 4 and 5. Dick Bate is the coach of the England U16 national team and has also authored two books, 'Coaching Advanced Players' and 'The Sweeper'. The session was done indoors in a 25 x 45-yard area. When practicing outdoors, a larger area would be used.

Working With Strikers

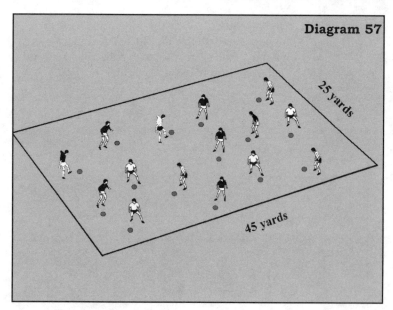

Diagram 57

Warm-Up

Organize the players with one ball each dribbling inside the grid doing the following:
- Dribble keeping head up and doing different fakes and moves
- Fake without touching the ball
- Start your dribble with two quick touches
- Start your dribble with two quick touches in different directions
- Fake and move by moving the ball

Coaching Point

Be convincing with your fakes.

Pass and Move

Organize the five players inside a 20 x 30-yard area with four players, each with a ball, on the perimeter. The five inside players move around and receive a pass from a perimeter player then pass to another perimeter player.

Coaching Points
- Stay away before asking for the pass - check away then come to receive the pass
- Show for the ball at the right time - when the passer has his head up
- When receiving the ball, keep your head up to look around - be aware
- After receiving the ball, pass to a perimeter player and move again looking for the return pass - give-and-go
- Try to play using one touch if possible
- If you use two touches, make them two quick touches
- Use different parts of your feet to receive and pass
- Experiment with different fakes and disguises with your receiving touch
- Do things that defenders wouldn't expect
- Let the ball run for someone else to receive if they shout "over" (Overs)

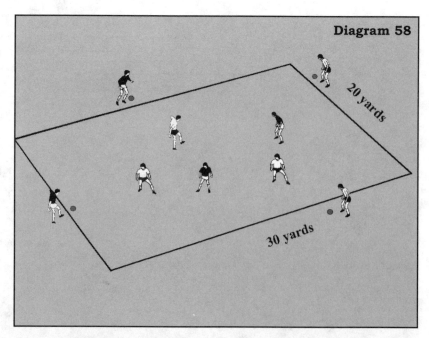

Diagram 58

Dick Bate

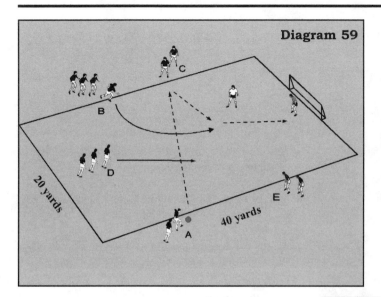

Diagram 59

Working To Goal

Organize the players in groups on a 20 x 40-yard area with a full size goal and goalkeeper.

Player A passes to incoming B.

Player C shouts "over" signaling B to let the ball roll by him.

Player C plays a one-touch pass into the path of B who has continued his run.

Player B shoots with one touch.

Progression

If the return pass from player C is poor or the defender blocks the shot, B can lay a pass off to D to shoot.

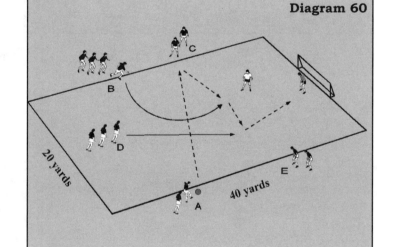

Diagram 60

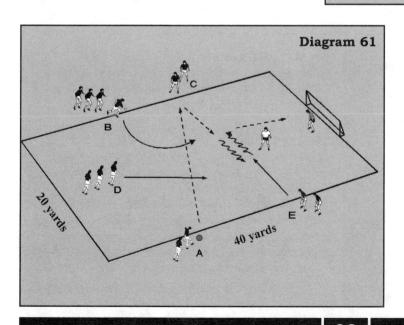

Diagram 61

Progression

If the defender blocks the pass from C to B, C can carry the ball across the field and try a takeover with E.

Coaching Points

• Carry the ball with the foot furthest away from the defender
• Use the words "take" for a takeover, "feet" for C to stop the ball for E to do a one-touch shot and "sole" for C to roll the ball back for E to shoot a moving ball
• Have the defender play passively to start

Chicago Fire

Observed during pre-season training in Ft. Lauderdale, February 2000.

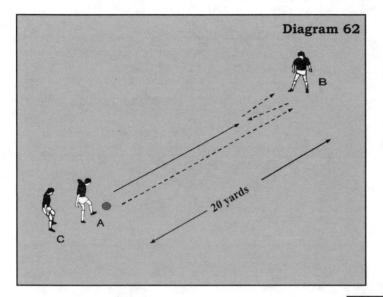

Diagram 62

Warm-Up

After 25 minutes of jogging and stretching, the players split into two groups. Group one is organized into groups of three with two players 20 yards apart from the third player as shown.
Player A passes to B and follows his pass.
Player B passes back with one touch to incoming A.
Player A passes the ball back to B at an angle with one touch.
Player B continues the drill by passing to C.

Progression

Extend the distance to 40 yards.

One v One To Goal

The players in group two played on a 35 x 20-yard field as shown with full size goals and goalkeepers. The first player in line A passes to B.
Player B receives the ball and attacks the goal that is defended by A.
Both players alternate lines.
Player D continues the drill by passing to C who attacks the opposite goal.

Coaching Point

Vary the service of the pass - low, high, driven, etc..

Diagram 63

Small-Sided Game

Group one then played 7 v 7 plus one neutral player on a 40 x 30-yard field with each team defending two small goals. Play four 5-minute games.

Observations

Head Coach Bob Bradley and assistant Frank Klopas played in the game and were instrumental in motivating the players throughout. I have observed a number of Bradley's practices and he has a knack of wringing every last drop of energy from his players. This game was no exception. With the teams tied in games won and goals scored, Bradley called for the outcome to be decided by a Golden Goal which got the players giving a 110% for the last few minutes before the winners were eventually decided.

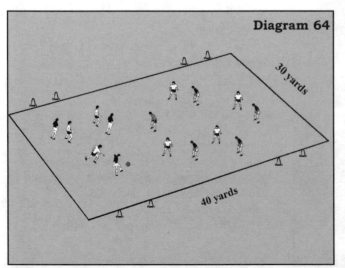

Diagram 64

Chicago Fire

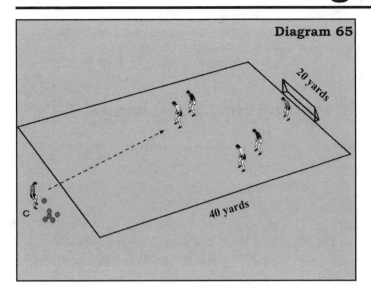

Diagram 65

One v One To Goal Progression

Group two continued with attacking and defending drills in a 40 x 20-yard field with one full size goal and goalkeeper. The coach has a supply of balls and passes across the field to the attackers (A). They attempt to turn and attack the goal defended by the defenders (D).

Coaching Point

The coach varies the service - low, in the air, driven, etc.

Progression

Group two progresses the drill by playing 2 v 2 to goal. The coach serves the ball in to either of the two forwards who attempt to turn and score. The forwards can either attempt to score on their own or combine with their partner.

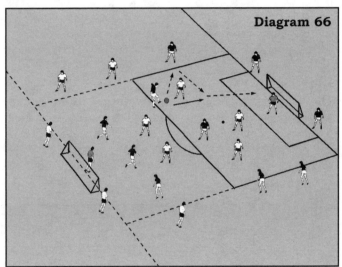

Diagram 66

Small-Sided Shooting Game

Both groups combine for the final game. Mark a field the size of two penalty areas with full size goals and goalkeepers. The players are organized into two teams of 10 and each team of 10 is split into two teams of five. Play 5 v 5 inside with each team having their other five teammates on the perimeter of the attacking half as shown. The players inside have unlimited touches. The perimeter players on the side have two touches and the players behind the goal have one touch. When a goal is scored, the team that concedes the goal alternates positions with their teammates on the perimeter.

Play for 15 minutes followed by 15 minutes of light jogging and stretching to cool down.

Diagram 67

Craig Brown

Craig Brown is the Manager/Coach of the Scotland National Team and is also the Technical Director of the Scottish Football Association. Previously he coached the Scotland U21 team to the U21 World Cup Finals.

Half Team Rotation - Crossing and Finishing

This is a one goal rotation training exercise which can be built up gradually into a functional exercise involving crossing and finishing in two ways:

A. Using a flat back four
B. Using a three man defense - two markers and a sweeper/libero

Initially, the exercise is set up as a training drill with pairs of players on the half-line. In wide positions there are two players on either side acting as wingers. The exercise begins with the player in possession on the half-line passing the ball to one of the strikers who has to play naturally from the time of receiving possession. Later, the strikers are taught movements such as 'across the face runs' that are introduced.

The ball must be passed on to a wide player who crosses for one of the two strikers or the opposite winger to shoot. A cross-over movement is an option on the way into the penalty box.

Rotation

The two midfield players now become wingers, the wingers become strikers and the strikers collect the ball and return to the midfield lines using the outside of the playing area. Fielders may be introduced, if appropriate, after the striking positions (i.e. midfield..winger..striker..fielder..midfielder).

The exercise can flow to one goal with as many players as the coach deems appropriate.

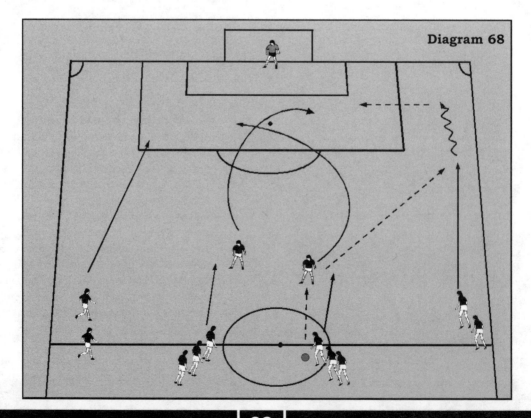

Diagram 68

Craig Brown

Introduction of Defenders

Once the basic movement in the box has been taught and appropriate delivery from wide positions has been achieved, one defender is introduced. He is asked to exaggerate his marking and pick up one of the three players coming in to receive the cross. Later, two defenders are introduced and given specific jobs.

Depending on the defensive system desired, either a sweeper/libero is brought into a defensive position or a back four is put in place. The defenders become 'active' whenever the wide player receives his first touch of the ball. At this point there is a 4 v 4 situation which makes it extremely difficult for the attacking players. Therefore, to support the attack, the midfield players go in behind the other four attackers. They position themselves as supporting midfield players, one on the side of the ball, and the other in a central position.

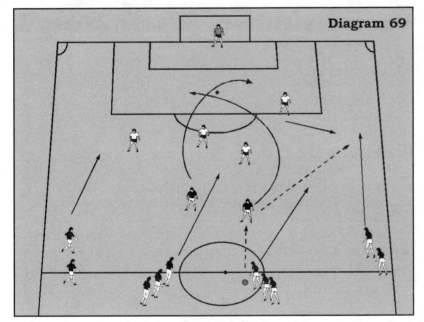

Diagram 69

Coaching Points - Attackers
- Possible additional cross over of strikers before arriving in the penalty box
- Early delivery from the wide players
- Choice of cross from the winger - near post, back post, over the top, cut back for midfielder
- Support from opposite wide player
- Nature of midfield support
- Response when possession is lost

Coaching Points - Defenders
- Fullback closing wide player quickly
- Holding the line
- No offside 'against the ball'
- The coordination of spaces between defenders
- Goalkeeper acting as sweeper
- Response when ball is played back or through defenders
- Action when possession is gained

Full Team Rotation

This is an exercise designed primarily for young players who are graduating from perhaps seven-a-side football to the full adult game. Having been encouraged not to play in a fixed position in the small-sided context, the players are given a 'feel' of all positions as they rotate in this format. It is of course a suitable game for senior players as it is an adaptation of SHADOW FOOTBALL which enables the coach to pattern certain playing movements.

The players are positioned on the pitch in a 4-4-2 shape with additional players positioned midway in their own half on the outside of the field on either side with a supply of balls. Three quarters of the pitch is used. The game starts with a throw in at the right back position. The ball is played quickly across the back four to the left back position and then to one of the two central midfield players. The midfielder then executes a pre-planned or spontaneous movement to the front or wide players. The team moves towards the opposing goal in an unopposed manner to finish with a shot. The two strikers then retrieve the ball and return to a fullback position on either side of the pitch.

Craig Brown

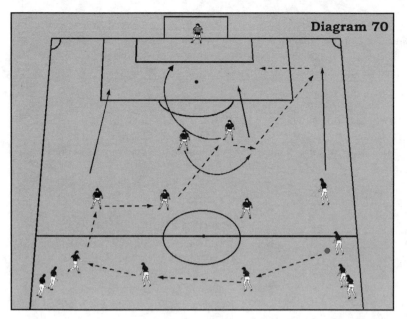

Diagram 70

Meanwhile the rotation is as follows: full back to center back, center back to center midfield, center midfield to wide midfield, wide midfield to striker, striker to fielder and fielder to full back. The entire team rotates in pairs and the shadow practice re-starts, this time from the opposite full back.

Later, two defenders then a back four can be added to make the practices more realistic. Waves of attack are then produced against opposing defenders, with the coach detailing the moves which he wishes to have executed.

Wingers Game

Using half a field, mark a channel down both flanks. Play 3 v 2 in each half. Position four wide players in the channels, two playing in the attacking half for each side. The objective is to play the ball from the back, where the three defenders should have comfortable possession against the two attackers, to a striker who passes wide to the unmarked winger. The cross is delivered to the two strikers, who, at the discretion of the coach, can be supported by one player 'breaking' from the back zone as well as the opposite winger, who, at this point, can come into the central area.

Whenever a goal is scored, or when the move breaks down, the players, or even the goalkeeper, play the ball wide to the unchallenged winger without it first going to one of the front two players. This makes the exercise easier for the less accomplished players.

Much coaching of all aspects of group play is possible, but particular emphasis should be placed on the type of crosses and the movement of the two forwards.

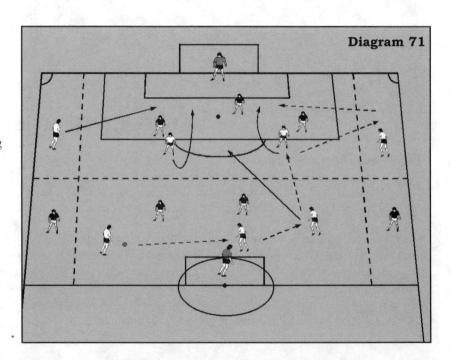

Diagram 71

Tampa Bay Mutiny

Observed in Florida, February 2000, during pre-season training.

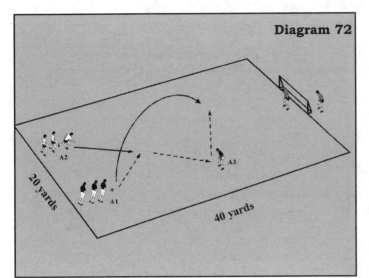

Diagram 72

Shooting/Finishing

A1 passes to A2.

A1 then makes an overlapping run.

A2 plays the pass to A3, who plays it into the path of overlapping A1 for the shot.

Players then rotate.

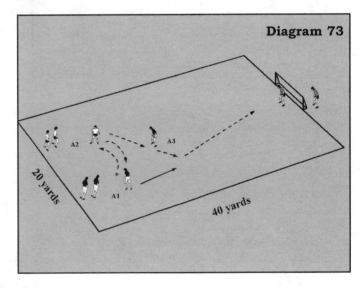

Diagram 73

Shooting/Volleys

A1 and A2 juggle the ball in the air back and forth towards A3.

When they are about five yards from A3, they pass the ball to him in the air.

A3 lays the ball off for either A1 or A2 to volley.

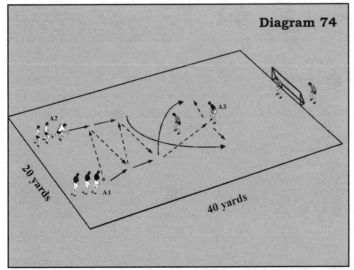

Diagram 74

Shooting/Finishing

A1 and A2 pass back and forth 3 or 4 times, then A2 runs past the defender.

A1 then passes to A3, who lays the ball off to either A1 or A2 to shoot with one touch.

Thailand National Team

Contributed by Thailand National Team Coach, Peter Withe. Withe had an outstanding playing career which included a European Cup Championship while at the English Premier League team, Aston Villa. Prior to taking the Thailand National Team position, Withe was coaching at Aston Villa in the English Premier League.

This is part one of an article that focuses on shooting. In all the exercises, an element of competition was incorporated by keeping score between two teams. Part two is the progression into games using a full field and will appear in the Jan/Feb 2001 issue.

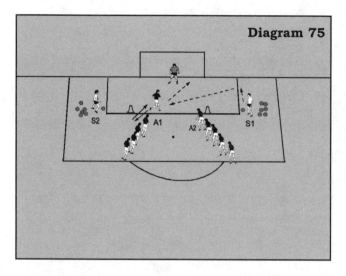

Diagram 75

Shooting

The players line up in two lines behind cones that are positioned on the six-yard line. Two coaches or servers are placed on the corner of the six-yard box with a supply of balls as shown in diagram 75. Server S1 triggers the start of A1's run by touching the ball forward. S1 then serves the ball for incoming A1 to shoot. After the shot, the players run behind the goal and join the back of the other line. The players must finish with their right foot from the right side and left foot from the left side.

Shooting

The same organization as in diagram 75 is used, except this time the players and servers are lined up 12 yards from goal.

Coaching Points

- Quality of shot - must hit the target
- Shoot with your instep
- Focus on making good contact with the ball
- The server must trigger the shooter's run by touching the ball forward before he crosses
- The players should check away to lose an imaginary marker before making their run

Diagram 76

Shooting

Again, use the same organization as in diagram 75, except this time the players and servers are lined up 18 yards from goal.

Coaching Point

The further from goal you are, the more you have to focus on hitting the target.

Note: If the players don't focus on the correct technique and hitting the target, they will miss shots even from six yards out.

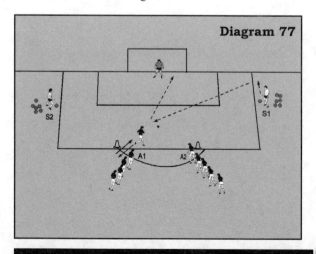

Diagram 77

Thailand National Team

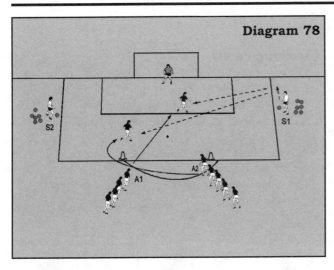

Diagram 78

Shooting In Pairs

Use the same organization as in diagram 77, however this time the players from line A1 and A2 run in pairs. A1 makes a near post run and A2 runs around A1's cone toward the far post. Doing this will stagger the incoming runs of the players so that A1 will be close to the six-yard line while A2 will be around 12-15 yards from goal when the cross comes in. The server has the option of which player he crosses to.

Progressions

All the previous drills can be used with volleys and headers.

Shooting

Organize a group of players behind each goal in a 50 x 30-yard area as shown in diagram 79. Use full size goals and goalkeepers. Player A1 touches the ball forward then hits a long diagonal pass to player A2. A2 controls the ball and runs with it until he reaches the half-line. He then passes to A1 who, after passing the ball, sprinted to a position about 20 yards from goal to receive the pass from A2. A1 passes back with one touch for A2 to shoot on goal. Repeat from the opposite end.

Coaching Points

- Quality of passes
- Player A1 moves quickly to 20 yards from goal, then gets his body in a side-on position and moves away from the ball until A2 is ready to pass
- Player A2 needs to judge the flight of the ball and control it at it's highest point with his chest or foot
- Look for rebounds
- Play from both ends and the left and right sides of the goal

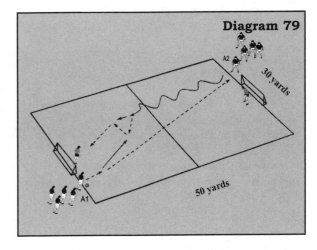

Diagram 79

30 yards

50 yards

Shooting

Use the same organization as in diagram 79 with the addition of two players, A2 and A3, who are positioned either side of the half-line as shown in diagram 80. The exercise starts with player A1 touching the ball out of his feet and passing to A2. A1 then follows his pass to support A2 and get the return pass. Before receiving the pass from A1, A2 moves away from the ball and then checks back to receive the pass and lays a one-touch pass back to A1. A1 passes to A3 who also moves away from the ball until it is passed, then checks back to receive the pass. A3 holds the ball until A2, who started his run following his pass to A1, is in a good position to shoot and then passes into the path of A2 who shoots with one touch. A3 is encouraged to look for rebounds. A1 takes A2's position, A2 takes A3's position and A3 joins the back of the opposite line.

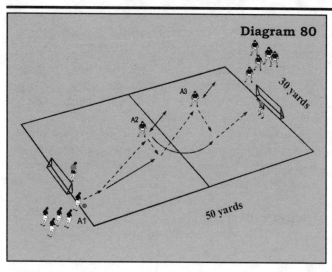

Diagram 80

Coaching Points

- Quality of passes
- A2 and A3 should move away then check back to receive the ball to lose their imaginary marker
- A2 should wait for A1 to pass to A3 before making his run
- A2's run should offer a good angle of support
- Hit the target with your shot
- Play from both ends and the left and right sides of the goal

Shooting

On a 50 x 40-yard field with full size goals and goalkeepers, organize the players as shown in diagram 81. Player A1 starts by touching the ball forward and then passing to A2. A2 attacks the ball and is joined by A3 who then play 2 v 1 against player A1 who follows his pass and defends his goal. This exercise can be used for 1 v 1, 2 v 1, 2 v 2, 3 v 2 or 3 v 3. It is also a good exercise to work with defenders.

Coaching Points

- Player A2 should get in line with the flight of the ball and attack it with his first touch
- Following his pass, A1 should move out quickly to pressure the ball
- Player A3 should time his run well - don't get ahead of A2 or lag too far behind
- Hit the target with your shot
- Play from both ends and the left and right sides of the goal

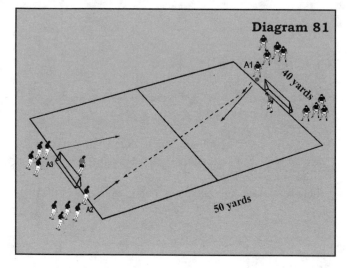

Diagram 81

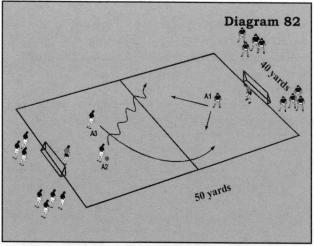

Diagram 82

Shooting

Diagram 82 is a continuance of the exercise in diagram 81. Once in possession of the ball, player A2 will take the ball wide and A3 will make his run to the opposite flank. This will allow A2 to shoot if A1 doesn't cover him or pass to A3 if A1 moves to cover him and stop any shooting opportunities by A2.

Training U14 Girls

Contributed by Jeff Pill, U.S. Women's National Staff Coach, U.S. Women's U18 National Team Assistant Coach and U14 Region One Director of Coaching. The following practices are part of the curriculum of the Region One U14 Girls ODP camp. You can find more of Jeff's training sessions at www.eteamz.com/soccer/pills/jpill.htm

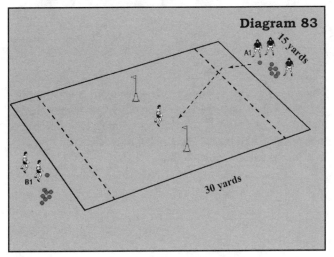

Diagram 83

Central Goal Shooting

Place flags to mark a goal in the middle of a 30 x 15-yard area as shown in diagram 83. Organize a team of three players at each end-line with a supply of balls. Player A1 touches the ball forward then shoots at the goal. A1 then follows his shot into the goal to be the goalkeeper for the next shot from B1 at the opposite end. The drill continues with shots alternating from each end.

Coaching Points

- Correct shooting technique - toe pointed, ankle locked, plant foot, follow through
- Use different surfaces to bend the ball

Zone Shooting

On a 40 x 30-yard field with full size goals and goalkeepers, play four defenders and two forwards in each half. The objective of the game is to look for shooting opportunities. Teams are awarded two points if they score from their defending half and one point if they score from the attacking half.

Coaching Points

- Team shape
- Keep the ball moving
- Think ahead - get in good shooting positions

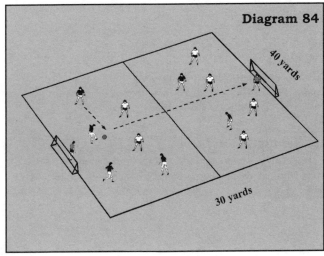

Diagram 84

Diagram 85

4 v 4 With Target Players

Organize three teams of four with two teams playing 4 v 4. The other team has a player on each side of the goal who act as target players for the team in possession. When one team scores, they then quickly try to attack the opposite goal. At this time, the losing team leaves the field and switches places with the target players who now enter the field.

End practice with a conditioned game with an emphasis on: team shape, correct shooting technique and finishing decisions.

Nottingham Forest U11 Team

Contributed by Peter Cooper, Nottingham Forest youth team coach. Cooper has coached youth players of different ages both at Nottingham Forest and Leeds United. This article focuses on cross-over runs and shooting. The size of the practice areas can be adapted depending on the age and skill level of the players.

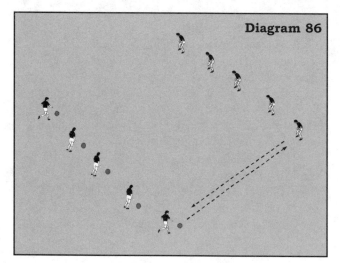

Diagram 86

Warm-Up

The players stand in pairs opposite each other. One player has a ball. The players pass to each other with conditions placed as to the number of touches they must have before they pass the ball back. The number of touches can start at five and be reduced down to one.

Warm-Up

The receiving player now runs to the middle to receive the pass. He then dribbles back to his cone and executes a turn before passing to his partner who does the same.

Coaching Points.

The receiving player should receive the ball on his back foot with a side-on stance, therefore receiving the ball half turned.

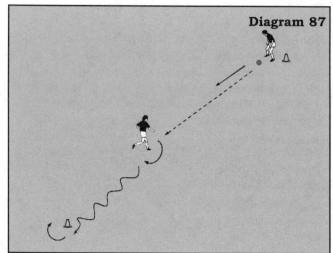

Diagram 87

Diagram 88

Shooting With Cross-Over Runs

The players line up in pairs. Player B has possession of the ball. A server is positioned 15-20 yards from goal. Player B passes to the server. Both players then make a cross-over run around the server. The server lays the ball off to player A who can shoot or cross for player B to shoot.

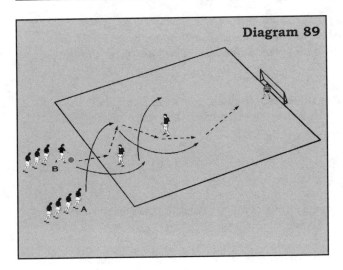

Diagram 89

Progression

Use the same organization as in diagram 88 except add a second server and perform two cross-over runs.

Coaching Point

Each server can lay the ball off to either player A or B

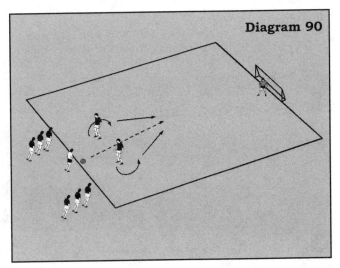

Diagram 90

1 v 1 Shooting

The players stand in pairs with their back to the goal and facing the server. The server passes a ball in between the two players who turn and fight for possession of the ball and to shoot.

Thailand National Team

Contributed by Thailand National Team Coach, Peter Withe. Withe had an outstanding playing career, which included a European Cup Championship while at the English Premier League team, Aston Villa. Prior to taking the Thailand National Team position, Withe coached at a number of clubs including Wimbledon and Aston Villa of the English Premier League.

This is part two of a two-part article that focuses on shooting. In all the exercises, an element of competition was incorporated by keeping score between two teams. Part one of this article appeared in the November/December 2000 issue.

9 v 9 Offside Shooting

I devised this practice to solve the problems I had with players having a tendency to run too early and thus into an offside position to receive a pass, plus to teach players to pass the ball into space rather than to the player.

The practice is 9 v 9 in the middle third of a full field that is marked into thirds with lines also extending from the penalty area as shown in diagram 91. Two coaches are positioned on the lines to see if a player runs into an offside position. The game starts with a coach serving the ball to the dark team who has to make a minimum of three passes before they can pass over the line and into space for a teammate who then goes 1 v 1 against the goalkeeper. Following an attempt at goal, the coach serves a ball to the white team and the game continues.

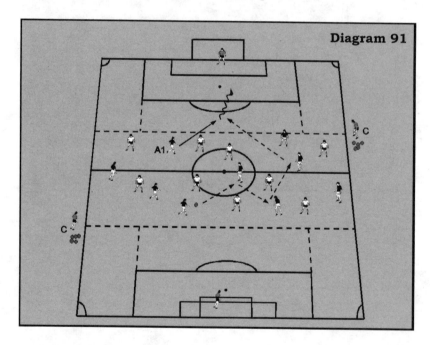

Diagram 91

Points Of Observation

The following are the tendencies of the players that this practice will help overcome.

- Rushing the final pass
- Attempting the final pass even when the opportunity is not there
- Play tends to be squeezed in a tight area instead of using the full width of the field
- The final pass is played to the player instead of to space
- The running player (A1) will run too early - offside
- The running player (A1) will run to the wrong area

Coaching Points

- Keep possession until you have a good opportunity to make a quality through-pass into the final third - even if this takes 6, 7 or 8 or more passes
- The timing and weight of the pass is critical - too hard and it will run out-of-bounds - too soft and it could be intercepted
- The timing of the run by A1 should allow him to get to the ball without running offside
- Use the entire area to keep possession and stretch the defending team - this will also open up gaps to make the final pass through

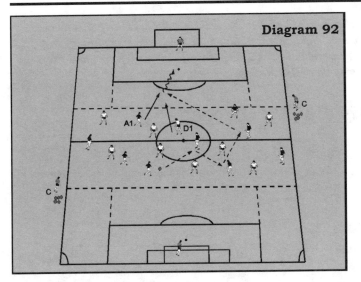

Diagram 92

Progression

Introduce a chasing defender (D1) who can chase A1 once he has touched the ball.

9 v 9 Crossing And Finishing

The same organization as the previous game except this time the final pass is played into the wide area for A3 who attacks the end-line and crosses for two players, A1 and A2 who have made runs into the penalty area.

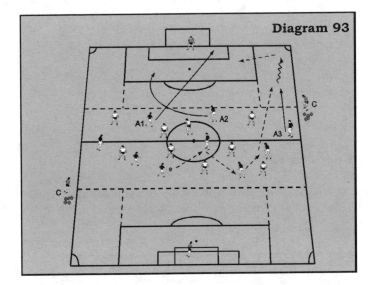

Diagram 93

Coaching Points

- All previous coaching points including timing of runs and weight of passes
- Players A1 and A2 should time their runs so they don't arrive too early
- Players A1 and A2 should stagger their runs as shown, with A1's near post run arriving first and A2's far post run arriving second
- Hit the target with the shot

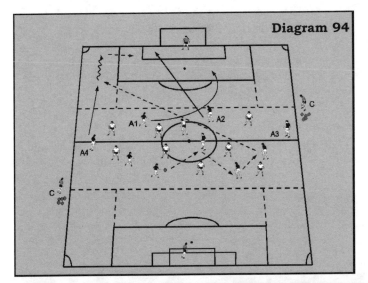

Diagram 94

Variation

The final pass can be made to the opposite flank area to A4 as shown in diagram 94.

A conditioning element can be introduced by asking A1, A2, A3 and A4 to make recovery runs back into the middle third playing area as quickly as possible. To make this effective, the coach should serve a ball back into play as soon as the players have made their attempt on goal.

Manchester United U19's

Contributed by Manchester United U19 coach, David Williams. Williams has extensive coaching experience and credentials including coaching in the English Premier League and at the National team level. Prior to joining Manchester United, Williams was the Assistant Manager/First Team Coach at Leeds United, Norwich City and Everton of the English Premier League and the Assistant Manager of the Welsh National Team.

Shooting From Square Passes

Most shooting sessions are set up where the player moves forward onto the ball to shoot at goal. It is important that players receive practice at shooting where they receive the ball from different angles. This shooting practice involves receiving the ball from square passes and shooting on the second touch.

Shooting

Organize two full-size goals and goalkeepers that are 36 yards apart (two penalty areas). The players in line A shoot to goal one and the players in line B shoot to goal two. Player A1 receives a pass facing his line. He has to receive and shoot using only his right foot and in two touches. Player B does the same. The shooter then joins the back of his line and is replaced by the passer.

Reverse the practice with player A1 shooting to goal two and player B1 shooting to goal one. They will then control and shoot the ball with their left foot.

Coaching Point

Remember, the players are only 18-20 yards from goal, so encourage a short, quick first touch as this will be required in game situations close to a crowded penalty area.

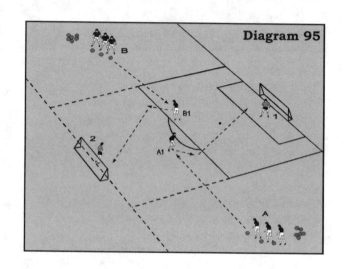

Diagram 95

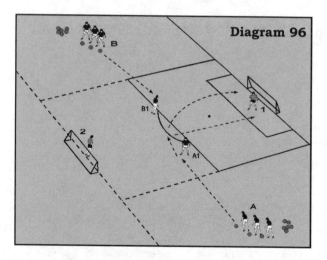

Diagram 96

Shooting

This time the shooter has his back to goal (side-on to the passer). The shooter allows the ball to go across his body to be controlled with his right foot and shoot with his left foot.

Reverse the practice with player A1 shooting to goal two and player B1 shooting to goal one. They will then control the ball with their left and shoot with their right foot.

Coaching Point

The shots could either be curled toward the far post or hit hard and low toward the near post as shown in diagram 96.

Brazilian Youth Practices

Submitted by Vinicius Dos Santos. The following practices were observed at the Clube Pequeninos Do Jockey, São Paulo, Brazil. Clube Pequeninos Do Jockey is a major youth soccer development program similar to the Tahuichi program in Bolivia. Pequeninos has relationships with many Brazilian, South American and even European Clubs. Their main function is to search and develop new talent for its clubs. Many professional players started their careers at Pequeninos including Ze Roberto of Bayer Leverkussen and the Brazilian National Team. Pequeninos is basically an inner city program. They have around 2,000 players aged 5 - 20 and almost 100 coaches. The following is a two-hour training session done with the U14/15 age group.

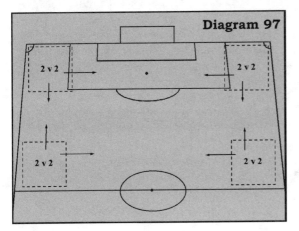

Diagram 97

Warm-Up
Upper and lower body coordination movements, lateral runs, zigzag runs, backward runs and stretches.

Technical
Mark four 15 x 15-yard areas, one in each corner of a half-field as shown in diagram 97. Organize the players into two teams of eight, one dark team and one light team. Play 2 v 2 keep-away in each 15-yard area. On the coach's whistle the groups rotate boxes as fast as they can. The dark team moves in a clockwise direction and the light team moves in a counter-clockwise direction. The objective is to get to the other box first and get possession of the ball. Play for 25 minutes.

Crossing and Finishing
These drills are practiced on a half-field. The idea is to attack with players coming from behind and by the flanks. It is very similar to the attacking style of the Second Division team AD São Caetano of São Paulo that made the finals of the Brazilian Competition JOAO HAVELANGE CUP 2000 against Vasco Da Gama of Rio de Janeiro (Romario`s team). AD São Caetano attacks by the flanks and constantly rotates the players as in a Futsal game (indoor soccer, not American indoor soccer). The fullbacks pass the ball and move forward into the space, the forwards come back to receive the ball, the midfielders use the space left by the forwards and the center defenders move forward to join the attack and so on. Once the players get to a certain space, they start their movement again. The movement should be fast and confident towards the goal, without forcing the play. This style requires excellent technical skills and ball control. The following examples are practiced without opposition at the start, then defenders are added to provide game-like opposition. When shooting on goal, the forwards start by having two touches and progress to finishing with one touch.

Crossing and Finishing
The midfielder starts with the ball and passes to the moving center defender.
The center defender passes to the fullback and then makes a run to the far post area.
The fullback passes quickly to the midfielder and then runs down the flank.
The midfielder plays a quick give-and-go with the forward, passes the ball into the path of the running fullback and then moves forward into a supporting position.
The forward runs around the two cones and into the penalty area to get on the receiving end of the cross from the fullback.
Continue the drill using the other flank. Each position has one or two back-up players.

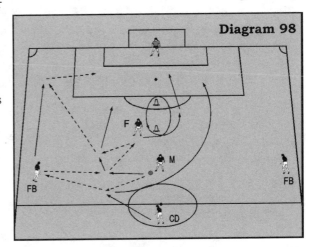

Diagram 98

Coaching Point
The cross has to be quick and direct - in games this won't allow the defenders time to get organized

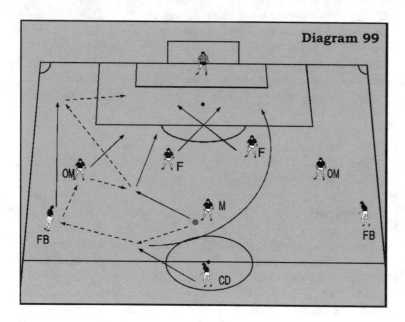

Diagram 99

Crossing and Finishing

Use the same organization as in diagram 98 with the addition of two outside midfielders and another forward.

The midfielder starts with the ball and passes to the moving center defender.

The center defender passes to the fullback and then makes a run to the far post area.

The fullback passes forward to the outside midfielder and then makes an overlapping run.

The outside midfielder passes inside to the incoming midfielder and moves forward into a supporting position.

The midfielder passes into the path of the overlapping fullback and moves forward into a supporting position

The two forwards make crossover runs into the penalty area at the time the fullback is about to cross the ball.

AD São Caetano

This is an example of a goal scored by AD São Caetano illustrating how the crossing and finishing rotations can work. The center defender is Ailton, the midfielder is Esquerdinha, the fullback is Cesar, forward 1 is Adhemar and forward 2 is Zinho.

AD São Caetano

Esquerdinha passes the ball to the moving Ailton who passes to Cesar and makes a run toward the far post area.

Cesar passes to the incoming Adhemar and makes a run down the flank.

Adhemar passes inside to Esquerdinha then makes a supporting run.

Esquerdinha passes wide into the path of the running Cesar then makes a supporting run.

Zinho moves into the space vacated by Adhemar and receives a pass from Cesar.

Zinho then passes to Esquerdinha who has moved into the space vacated by Zinho.

Esquerdinha passes into the path of the Ailton who made his run from a deep position and wasn't picked up by the defenders.

Ailton took his shot from the edge of the penalty area and scored.

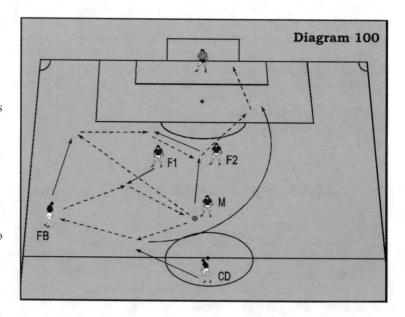

Diagram 100

Brazilian Youth Practices

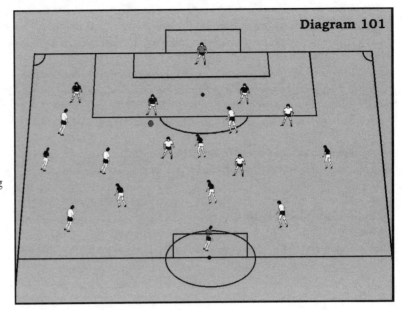

Diagram 101

Half-Field Game

Organize two teams of eight on a half-field with full size goals and goalkeepers. The dark team starts as the attacking team and can score in either goal. The light team is the defending team and aims to keep possession when they have the ball. The defending team can pass to the goalkeepers making it 10 v 8. Play four 5-minute quarters with the teams alternating roles each quarter.

Cool Down

Practice ended with a barefoot jog around the field and stretches.

Barnsley F.C.

Contributed by long-time subscriber Gerry Canavan. Ten years ago at the age of 15 Gerry spent the summer training with Sheffield United, then in the English Premier League. At the time, Dave Bassett was the manager of Sheffield United. Over the last 10 years Gerry has been fortunate to visit Bassett as his coaching career has taken him to Nottingham Forest and now, Barnsley F.C. of the English First Division. In 2000, Gerry spent six weeks at Barnsley F.C. observing practices of all the teams and even training with the youth and reserve teams as well as helping to coach the younger Academy players. Gerry also traveled with the players and coaching staff as he observed the games of the first team, reserves and youth teams. Gerry is an active coach (USSF "B" License and NSCAA Advanced Diploma) in his home town of Chicago where he is Director of Coaching for the Wilmette Wings S.C.

Gerry would like to thank Barnsley F.C., Dave Bassett, John Greaves, Derek French and all of the coaching staff and players for their hospitality and kindness over his six-week stay.

Crossing and Finishing

Almost every training session finishes with some sort of shooting or crossing and finishing exercise, especially for forwards and midfielders. (There has to be some correlation with the fact that Barnsley has scored even more goals than Manchester United at this point of the season.)

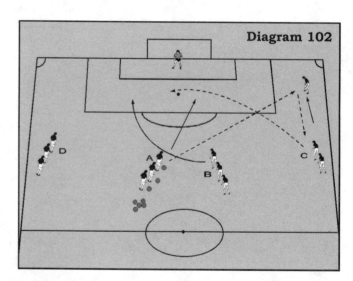

Organize four lines of players as shown in diagram 102. Player A serves a ball diagonally for player C to run on to. Players A and B then make crossover runs into the penalty area. Player C sets the ball backwards with one touch if possible for the next player in line to cross with one touch. Repeat with opposite flank.

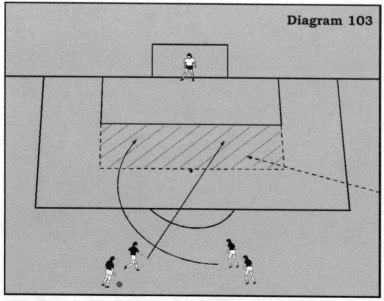

Coaching Points

- The near post run should come from the furthest forward, and the closer forward should loop around to the far post
- The cross should be aimed into an "imaginary" 6 yard target area located between the 6-yard line to the penalty spot
- Crosses should be driven hard and accurate

Newcastle United U17 & U19

Contributed by Alan Irvine, Newcastle United Academy Director and coach of the Newcastle U17 and U19 youth teams. Irvine played professionally before moving into coaching. The following is a series of passing combinations that are practiced unopposed. Although the examples are shown working on one flank, they would be practiced by alternating flanks with each repetition. Two or three players would be lined up at each position. The forwards are positioned in a marked area as shown. You can also vary the positioning of the players to suit your playing formation and end each repetition with various finishing exercises. Defenders can be introduced gradually to make it more game realistic.

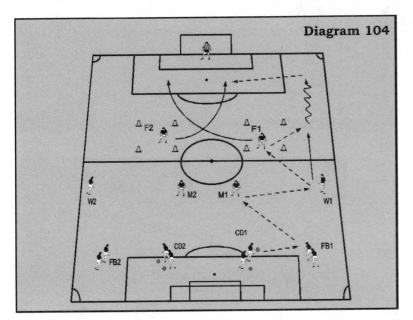

Diagram 104

Passing Combinations

CD1 passes to FB1.
FB1 passes to M1.
M1 passes to W1.
W1 plays a give-and-go with F1.
W1 attacks the endline and crosses for incoming F1 and F2.

Passing Combinations

The same as diagram 104, except the ball is switched from one flank to the other.
CD1 passes to FB1.
FB1 passes to M2.
M2 passes to W2.
W2 plays a give-and-go with F2.
W2 attacks the endline and crosses for incoming F1 and F2.

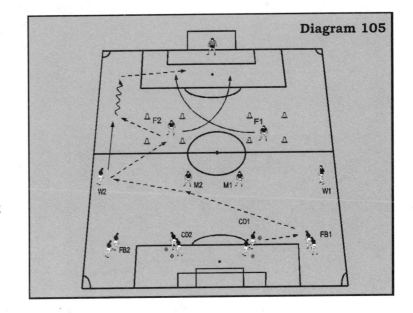

Diagram 105

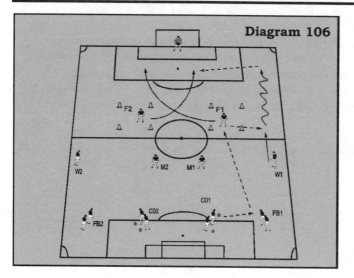

Diagram 106

Passing Combinations

CD1 passes to FB1.

FB1 passes to F1.

F1 passes wide to running W1.

W1 attacks the end-line and crosses for incoming F1 and F2.

Passing Combinations

CD1 passes to M1.

M1 passes to FB1.

FB1 passes to W1.

W1 passes to F1.

F1 lays the ball back to M1.

M1 passes into the path of running W1 who attacks the end-line and crosses for incoming F1 and F2.

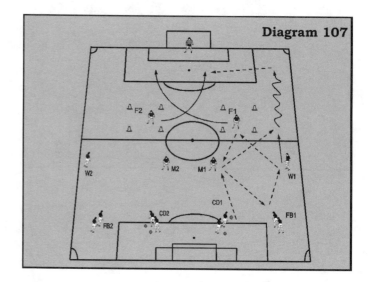

Diagram 107

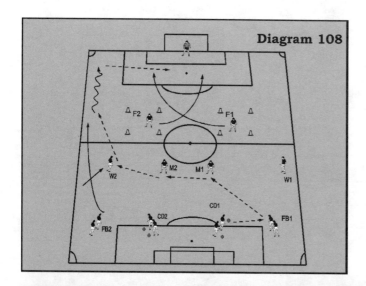

Diagram 108

Passing Combinations

CD1 passes to FB1.

FB1 passes to M1.

M1 passes to M2.

M2 switches flanks passing to W2.

W2 moves inside creating room on the flank for FB2 to make an overlapping run.

W2 passes into the path of overlapping FB2.

FB2 attacks the end-line and crosses for incoming F1 and F2.

Barnsley F.C.

Contributed by long-time subscriber Gerry Canavan. In 2000, Gerry spent six weeks at Barnsley F.C. observing practices of all the teams and even training with the youth and reserve teams as well as helping to coach the younger Academy players. Gerry also traveled with the players and coaching staff as he observed the games of the first team, reserves and youth teams. Gerry is an active coach (USSF "A" License and NSCAA Advanced Diploma) in his home town of Chicago where he is Director of Coaching for the Wilmette Wings S.C.

Thursday: Warm-Up

The players jog and stretch for about 20 minutes while the coach, Dave Bassett, is out on the training pitch setting up the session. The session focuses on linking up play in the middle third and getting midfielders or forwards to run in behind the defense.

Organization: 10 v 10

The two teams must play between the offside lines (which can be coned or marked off). Both teams are shaped into a 4-3-2 formation with goalkeepers. The goalkeepers serve the ball in to the forwards to start play. If the combination play releases a player up the middle, then they have one touch to control and another touch to finish. (A one-touch finish is encouraged as the session progresses.) If the combination play releases a player out wide, then another player can run freely into the penalty area and score from the resulting cross.

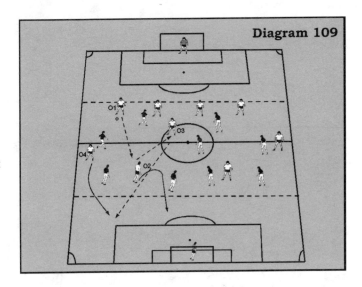

Diagram 109

Coaching Points

- Timing of the runs in behind the defense or across a defender is the key to success

Breakdown

The basic pattern as seen in diagrams 109 and 110 is to play the ball up to a striker, lay it back and then play it through into the space. Diagrams 109 and 110 concentrate on passing the ball wide. In diagram 109 , O1 plays the ball to O2 (a forward). O2 sets it back to O3 and spins to the middle to make space for O3 to pass the ball through (either over the top or through a gap) for O4 to run onto. O4 must time his run and stay on-side before delivering a cross to O2, who has spun inside following his pass.

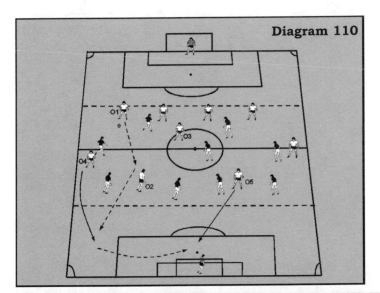

Diagram 110

Coaching Points

- The general pattern is encouraged continuously
- The midfielders and forwards were told to constantly run either behind or across the defense and defenders.

Variation

As shown in diagram 110, O2 can pass into the space wide for O4 in behind the fullback while O5, the other forward, makes his run to finish off the resulting cross.

Barnsley F.C.

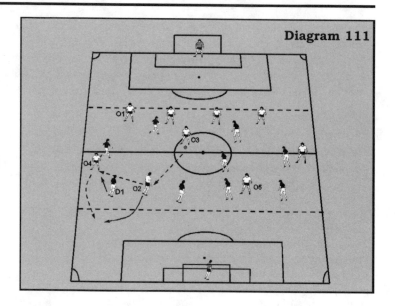

Diagram 111

Playing The Second Forward In

The example in diagram 111 shows O3 (the center midfielder) passing to O2 (the first forward). O2 sets the ball back and square to O4 (the wide player) which draws out D1 and creates space for O2 to attempt to make a run in behind.

Diagram 112

Making The Decision

In diagram 112, after playing the ball wide to O4, O2 pulls out wide, drawing D2 out wide with him and thus creating space in the center of the defense for O5 to run into. O4 has the choice of passing down the line to O2 or to wait and play a pass into the space where O2 has come from, to O5.

Playing The Midfielder In

In this example, after playing the ball wide to O4, O2 again pulls D2 wide creating space while O5 makes a looping run and cuts away from D3. D3 tracks O5's run and in doing so, creates even more space for O3 to exploit through the middle. O3 makes a timed run into the path of the pass from O4.

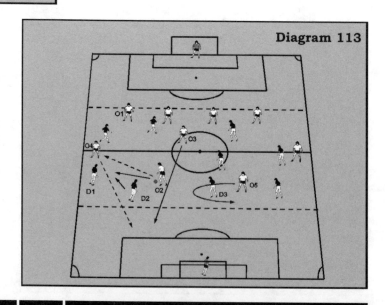

Diagram 113

Barnsley F.C.

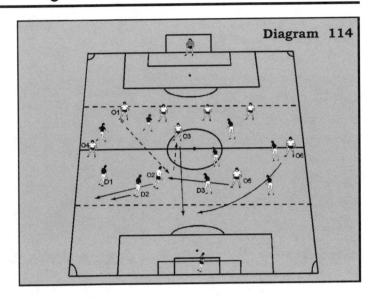

Diagram 114

Playing The Wide Midfielder In

In diagram 114, O1 starts with the ball and looks at the options available to him. O2 makes a run in behind D1 taking D2 with him. O5 moves into the space O2 has created and receives a pass from O1. O5 sets the ball back to O3 who plays the ball through to O6 who has drifted behind D3 and into the space left by O5.

Coaching Point

Timing of the runs in behind the defense or across a defender are the keys to success.

Diagram 115

Playing the Wide Midfielder In

In diagram 115, O1 starts with the ball and plays a long pass to O2. O2 receives the ball with his back to goal and sets it back to O3. O5 spins away and pulls D4 wide, creating space for O6 who's made a diagonal run in behind D4 to receive the ball from O3.

Coaching Points

• The midfielders and forwards were told to constantly run either behind or across the defense and defenders.
• Communication and decision making, coupled with quality timed passes, were the key to all the variations

AFC Manawatu - New Zealand

Contributed by Richard Hudson, head coach of the New Zealand First Division Team, AFC Manawatu. This article is a selection of exercises to improve shooting.

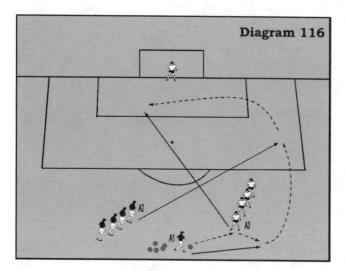

Diagram 116

Shooting Drill One

Using a half-field, A1 plays the ball to A3 then creates the angle to receive the ball back from A3. A1 then plays the ball down the wing for A2 who makes a diagonal run to either finish with one touch or to cross to A3 who has spun to get into the penalty area.

Coaching Points

• Good communication between the attackers
• Timing of passes
• Weight of passes
• Quality of the finish

Use both sides of the field and rotate the servers.

Shooting Drill Two

Working on a half field, four groups of players are positioned either side of each goal. (with four servers and two goalkeepers). A1 and A2 run from their respective ends at the same time to receive a pass from servers 1 and 2. Both A1 and A2 make a one-touch shot then join the players behind lines A3 and A4. The sequence continues with A3 and A4 receiving from servers 3 and 4.

Coaching Point

Good understanding between the attackers and servers is essential in the timing of passes in relation to the runs.

Diagram 117

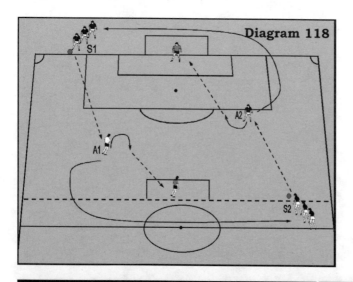

Diagram 118

Shooting Drill Three

Server 1 (S1) passes to A1 who turns with the ball and shoots. At the same time S2 passes to A2 who also turns with the ball and shoots. Once A1 and A2 have taken their shots, they join the opposite groups and the sequence continues.

Coaching Points

• Accuracy and weight of passes from S1 and S2
• A1 and A2 should fake before receiving the ball to turn and shoot
• Quality of A1 and A2's first touch
• Goalkeeper's position in relation to the attacker's position

Bodens BK - Sweden

Contributed by Bodens BK head coach Lars Svensson. Bodens BK play a version of the 4-4-2 formation that is played more as 3-1-1-2-1-2 formation. This article focuses on building attacks from an outside defender.

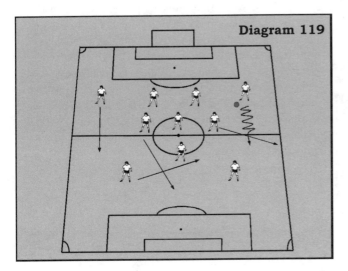

Building Up the Attack From the Fullback

If the left defender gains possession of the ball he should attack the space in front. The opposite fullback has the option to also move forward but normally he and the two center defenders stay and slide over towards the ball side (in this case to the left). As soon as the fullback attacks, the left midfielder should move out wide to the touch-line with the right sided forward moving infield to create space for the right midfielder to make diagonal runs in behind the opposition's fullback and central defender.

Finding Space

The attacking midfielders have to try to find space. Diagram 120 shows an option when the right defender starts with the ball. The fullback passes a long ball into the forward who lays it back to one of the offensive central midfielders. At the same time, the right midfielder should move out wide and as soon as the ball is played back, he then runs down the wing to receive a one-touch pass from the central midfielder. Play then develops with forwards and midfielders making runs into the penalty area to meet a cross delivered by the right midfielder.

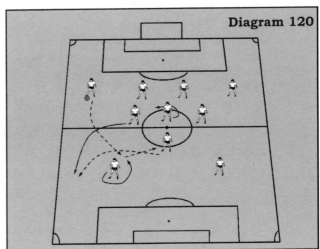

Variations

The right fullback passes the ball to a playmaker who creates space for himself. The playmaker then passes the ball forward with one touch to the offensive midfielder. The ball is then passed to the opposite fullback who is overlapping down the left wing. Play again develops with players spinning and making runs into the penalty area to receive a cross from the left fullback.

Bodens BK - Sweden

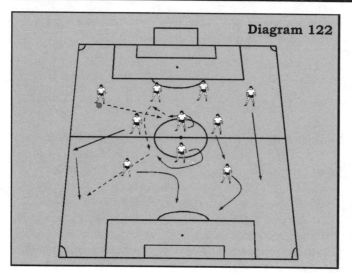

Diagram 122

Bringing Defenders Into Play

In this example, the right fullback passes the ball inside to the playmaker who lays it back, one touch, to one of the central defenders. The central defender then plays a forward pass to the offensive central midfielder who has made space for himself. With a one-touch pass, the central midfielder releases the ball to the right midfielder who has again moved wide. The left fullback continues his run down the left wing and becomes the third attacker looking to receive a cross into the penalty area from the wide right midfielder.

Switching the Point of Attack

In this example, the right fullback passes the ball into the playmaker. The playmaker turns and passes the ball wide to the left defender who has made a surging run down the wing. The fullback, upon receiving the ball, dribbles inside and then releases to the central midfielder who has made an overlapping run into space.

Play develops until a goalscoring opportunity is created.

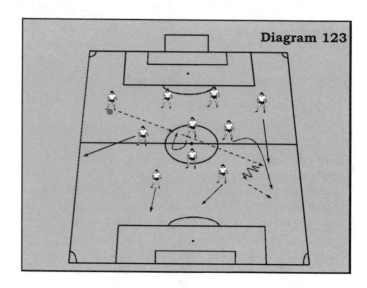

Diagram 123

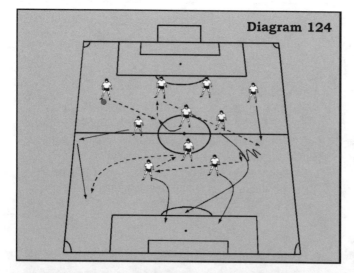

Diagram 124

Progression

The right fullback passes the ball to the playmaker who lays it off to the central defender. The central defender switches play and passes to the overlapping left defender. The left defender dribbles the ball inside and passes to the opposite target forward. The target forward lays it off first time to the offensive midfielder who then passes it one touch to the overlapping right midfielder who makes the final cross. Meeting that cross should be the two forwards and the other offensive midfielder. Backing them up should be the left fullback who continues to move forward with the play.

Bodens BK - Sweden

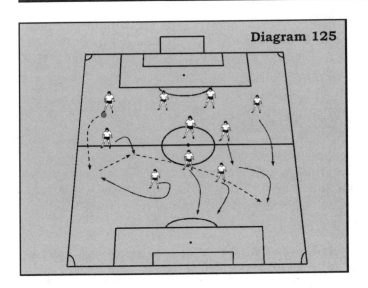

Diagram 125

Forward Runs

In this system of play it is essential that the forwards make deep runs in order to create space, not only for themselves, but also for the offensive midfielders. Alternatively they can also move towards the offensive midfielders and create space 'in behind' for the offensive midfielders to exploit with diagonal runs. In this variation, the forward peels wide to receive a pass from the right fullback and lays it back to the right midfielder who has moved inside to create space for that forward. The right midfielder then switches play and releases to the left midfielder who has moved out wide to deliver a cross. Play finishes following an attempt on goal.

Liverpool F.C.

During my visit to England in October 2000, I was fortunate to spend a day at Liverpool F.C. with Assistant Manager, Sammy Lee. This drill, done by the first team players was practices at the end of the training session.

Shooting Drill

This shooting drill is one-touch where X1 passes to X2 who passes to X3, to X4 to X5 who lays the ball into X3's path for a shot. Players rotate 1 to 2 to 3 to 4 to 5 to the X1 line.

Some of the group then finished with some head tennis while others (Robbie Fowler and the forwards) worked on some individual finishing.

The warm-down consisted of some light jogging and a stretch.

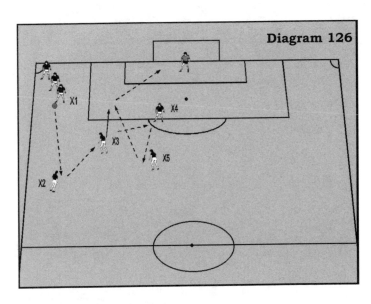

Diagram 126

Craig Brown

Craig Brown is the Scotland National Team head coach and Technical Director of the Scottish F.A. Craig is well known in the soccer community as one of the world's leading clinicians. We are pleased and feel fortunate to have Craig Brown as the featured clinician for our International Coaching Seminar in Kansas City on February 8 - 10, 2002. Visit our web site for further information.

Breaking From Midfield

Play 3 v 3 around the center circle in a 15 x 15-yard area. The required number of consecutive passes (say, four) has to be achieved before the ball can be played out to the side. At the side, and slightly behind the central box, is a line of right sided wide players ready to receive a pass played from the central box. The requirement is for the wide right player to play an early ball (first or second touch) to one of the two strikers positioned at the edge of the penalty area, and then go in wide support.

The two strikers, who are marked by two defenders, have the support of the wide player and one additional player breaking from the central 3 v 3 box. After the 4 v 2 attack is completed, the overlapping wide player returns to the end of the line and the supporting midfield player goes back to the 3 v 3 situation, which resumes in midfield.

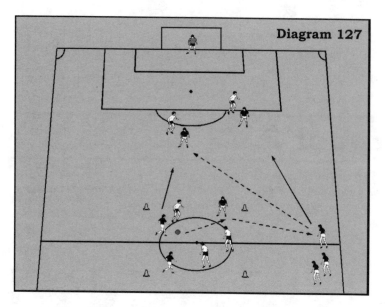

Diagram 127

Progressions

Clearly, adaptations of this basic arrangement are possible, particularly by introducing other groups of three in central midfield and then changing the overlapping side to the left. Also an additional defender (e.g. a sweeper or free defender) can be introduced.

Mick Hennigan

Mick Hennigan conducted this lively session on shooting at the WORLD CLASS COACHING International Coaching Seminar in Connecticut, June 2000. The session had an overall theme of "quality finishing" with an emphasis of shots hitting the target.

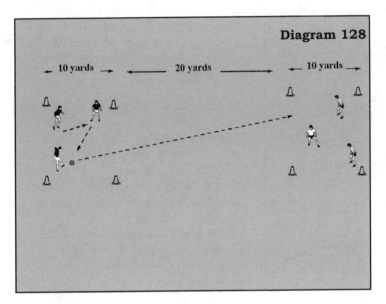

Diagram 128

← 10 yards →   ← 20 yards →   ← 10 yards →

Warm-Up
Organize two 10 x 10-yard grids that are 20 yards apart. Have three players in each grid. The players in one grid pass the ball around and then drive a firm pass into the other grid.

Coaching Points
- Each player must touch the ball once before it is passed into the other grid
- The pass must remain below head height
- Drive the pass into the other grid with the instep
- Focus and be on your toes so that you can make the correct decision of a short pass or a long pass into the other grid depending on how the ball comes to you

Progression
Instead of passing the ball into the other grid, now shoot it hard and low. If the other team can't control the ball and keep it in their grid, you win a point.

Goalbox Shooting
The practice area is the 18-yard goalbox marked out as shown with another goal positioned on the 18-yard line. Organize four groups of shooters at each goal post as shown in diagram 129. Four servers should be outside the penalty area. Each server is responsible for passing to a specific shooting group, e.g. S1 to A1 and S2 to A2, etc. The exercise starts with S1 dribbling the ball and then passing into the goalbox on the ground for A1 to run in and shoot. Next S2 passes for A2 and so on.

Diagram 129

S3   A2   A3   S2

S1   A4   A1   S4

Progression
Add goalkeepers and the servers can now cross the ball for volleys and headers.

Coaching Points
- Attack the ball
- Don't kill your space by getting there too early
- Shoot back to the direction the ball came from
- Wait until the last moment to attack the ball
- Communication between wide players and strikers

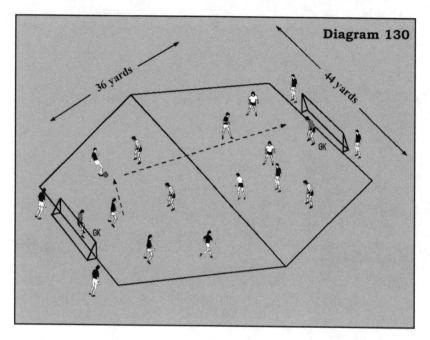

Diagram 130

Diamond Shooting

The field in diagram 130 is 36 x 44 yards. However, the sidelines are tapered in toward each goal giving a diamond-type shape. This stops the players from taking the ball out wide and taking shots from difficult angles.

Balls are placed in each goal with a player at each side of the goal to retrieve balls. Players are organized into 4 v 2 in each half. Players can only stay in their own half of the field. The four players can only score from their own half of the field. The two forwards can follow in for rebounds. Goalkeepers can only pass the ball into their own half. Defenders are limited to two-touch and any player that shoots the ball over the crossbar is replaced by one of the fielders.

Coaching Points
- Take the first shooting opportunity
- Attempt to shoot on the first-touch whenever possible
- Follow shots in for rebounds

Progressions
- Use one of the two forwards as a target man
- One of the four players can join the attacking half with the ball

Sammy Lee

This session by Sammy Lee was conducted at the WORLD CLASS COACHING International Coaching Seminar in Connecticut, June 2000 and starts with a circle warm-up, progresses to a small-sided passing game and finishes with a half-field game designed to get the ball wide for a cross.

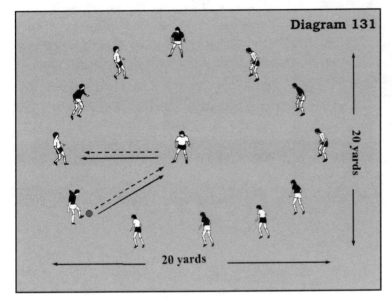

Diagram 131

20 yards

20 yards

Warm-Up

Organize the players into a 20-yard circle with one player in the center. The exercise starts with a player passing the ball to the center player and following his pass. The center player then passes the ball to the next player in a clockwise direction and follows his pass. The exercise continues round the circle

Progressions

- Play two-touch
- Play a give-and-go with the player on the outside
- After playing the give-and-go, pass to the next player

Coaching Points

- Angles are important
- Communication
- When on the perimeter, stay out of the circle, don't come to meet the pass and close down you space.

Small-Sided Game

In a 40 x 20-yard area, play 7 v 7 plus two neutral players that play for the team in possession. On each end-line is a target player. The objective is for the team in possession to pass the ball to the target player in the direction they are playing. If they are successful, the target player passes back to the same team who now attacks the opposite end.

Coaching Points

- Your team needs possession to get progression
- Encourage build-up play using moves learned in the warm up
- Be patient with your players, this is not an easy exercise

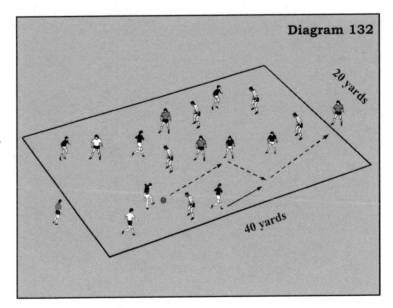

Diagram 132

20 yards

40 yards

Sammy Lee

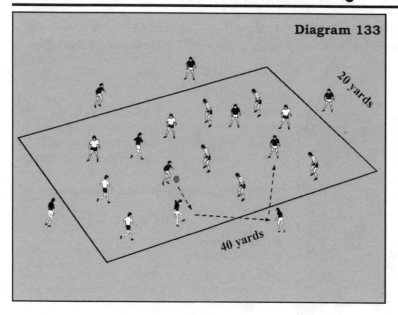

Diagram 133

20 yards

40 yards

Small-Sided Game

In the same 40 x 20-yard area, organize two teams of 10 players. One team plays with 10 players inside the area while the other team has five inside and five other players spaced on the perimeter. The objective of the game is to keep possession. The team with 10 players on the inside are limited to two-touch. The other team has unlimited touches for the inside players and the perimeter players are limited to one or two-touch. The teams change after every few minutes so each team takes turns having perimeter players.

Coaching Points
• Quality of passes and receiving touch
• Speed of play and decision making
• Perimeter players move to create angles and space

Half-Field Game

Extend the lines of the penalty area to the half-line as shown in diagram 134. Inside the marked area play eight attackers against five defenders. The objective is for the attacking team to play the ball into the wide channels to an overlapping player who attacks the end-line at full speed and crosses. Attacking players cannot stand in the wide channels waiting for a pass. They must enter once the pass has been made. Once the ball has been played wide, one defender and two attackers are allowed into the penalty area. If the defenders win possession they attempt to score in either of the two small goals (cones) on the half-line.

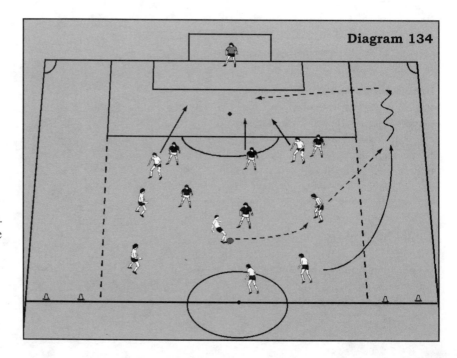

Diagram 134

Progression

Two of the attackers have colored jerseys and are allowed unlimited touches. The other six attackers are limited to two-touch. Once the ball is passed into the wide channels, everyone can enter the penalty area.

Sammy Lee

Sammy Lee conducted this session at the WORLD CLASS COACHING International Coaching Seminar in Connecticut, June 2000, which started with some fun warm-ups and progressed to various finishing exercises that included defenders as well as forwards shooting on goal. The final progression was a half-field game that included overlapping defenders pushing forward and overloading the attack.

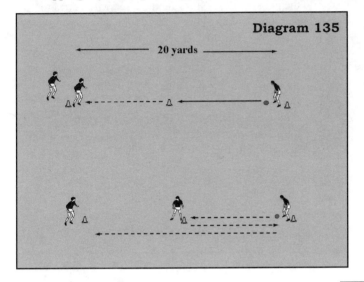

Warm-Up

Organize the players in groups of three with cones 20 yards apart and a cone between them in the middle. Warm-up with variations of dribbling, juggling and passing between the cones. Stretch every few minutes.

Head And Volley To Goal

Organize the players as shown in diagram 136. Player 1 throws the ball up and heads it to player 2. Player 2 heads the ball for player 1 to run onto and head for goal. The players rotate each time - player 1 goes to player 2's position and player 2 goes in goal. The player in goal joins the back of the line.

Coaching Points
• Cannot score in the six-yard area
• The quality of the set up header is vital

Progression
Start from 25-30 yards from goal with volleys instead of headers

Shooting

Organize the players as shown in diagram 137. Player 1 passes in to player 2 who lays the ball off for player 3, then gets a return pass from player 3 and shoots to score.

Coaching Points
• Shoot from outside the penalty area if possible
• The quality of the pass is vital to a good shot

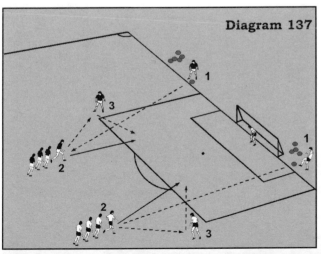

Sammy Lee

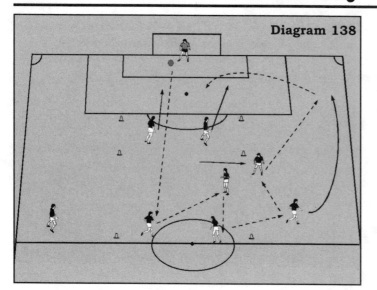

Diagram 138

Half-Field Combinations

Organize two strikers in a coned area just outside the penalty area. Mark another area with cones for four midfielders. Position two fullbacks in wide positions. The goalkeeper starts the exercise by kicking long into the square of four players. Once in possession the players attempt the same patterns and rotations as in the previous drills. In this example, the ball is played to the fullback who passes into a midfielder who has moved into a wide position, and makes an overlapping run, where he receives the ball to cross. The two strikers make runs into the penalty area.

Progression - "Over"

In the example in diagram 139, the fullback passes to the wide midfielder who lets it run by him to the forward who gave the shout, "over". The forward then plays the ball for the overlapping fullback.

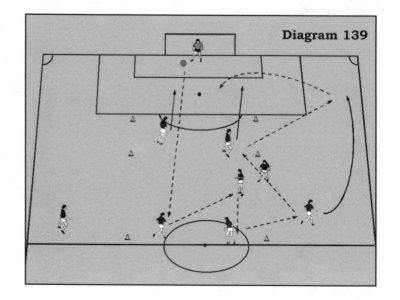

Diagram 139

Lira Lulea BK - Sweden

Contributed by Lars Svensson, head coach of Lira Lulea BK. Lars Svensson played soccer for over 17 years in his native country, Sweden, where he currently coaches the First Division club, Lira Lulea BK. Svenssons' background also includes coaching at the youth level. He is head of coaching for the Swedish High School Association. His other duties include head of talent scouting in the Northern District of Sweden for the Swedish Soccer Federation and Chief Coaching Instructor for the Northern District of Sweden.

I prefer to play a 4-3-3 formation with my teams in which I emphasize 'Speed of Movement'. The following training session is a series of attacking combinations that we practice to help the players become familiar with their roles.

The following are generic coaching points that I use for all training sessions to help my players understand my philosophy and the style of soccer I would like them to play:

• Movement before passing - be in a position to receive the ball - try to lose your marker
• Law of opposite movement - when one teammate moves toward you to receive the ball, at least one should move away to be open for the long pass
• Keep wide on the attacking flank but move inside if you are on the opposite flank
• If we attack on one flank, our weak side fullback

should take a more central position behind the person in possession - this is a good position if we decide to switch flanks or if we lose possession
• When we switch flanks, we should do it with a quick tempo - few touches and quick movement
• Once the ball is wide, expect a cross - two players should attack the central and near post area and the weak side forward should attack the far post area.
• Attack as a team - the defenders should push the whole team up when attacking
• Every player should be looking to support the player in possession of the ball
• When we have the ball, other players should:
    Try to get behind the defensive line.
    Find the space in front of the defense and behind the midfielders.

Combination One

The ball is played in from the coach to player A1 who is in a wide position. A1 attacks the end-line to a position where he can make a cross. Players A2, A3 & A4 make runs into the penalty area in an attempt to score.

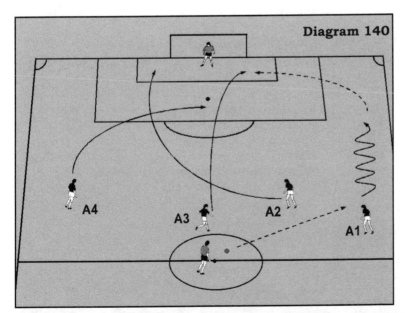

Runs made by attacking players

A2 runs to the far post.
A3 runs to the near post.
A4 runs to the penalty spot.

Coaching Points

• The drill should be done as quickly as possible
• Attacking players must get into the area as soon as they can
• Timing of the run is important
• Quality of crosses

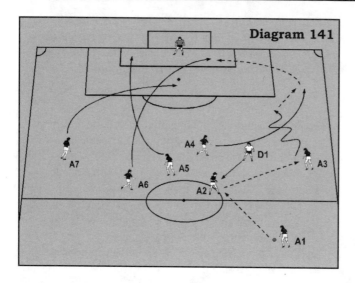

Diagram 141

Combination Two

Player A1 passes the ball to Midfielder A2.
A2 will attract the defender D1 by moving inside and toward the passer creating space on the flank for A3.
A2 passes with one touch to A3.
A3 dribbles the ball until A4 has made an overlapping run.
A3 then plays the ball to A4 to cross.
The three other attacking players will make runs into the area as in combination one.

Coaching Points

- A2 must pass one-touch wide to A3
- A4 must get the timing of his run correct
- Timing of runs toward goal are important

Combination Three

Player A2 moves inside and toward the passer taking defender D1 with him as in combination two. This creates space for A1 to pass to the forward A3.
A3 lays the ball off to A4 who started his run when A1 made the initial pass.
A4 passes the ball wide to A5 and continues his run into an attacking position.
A5 attacks the end-line and crosses.
A3, A4 and A6 then make their runs into penalty area.

Coaching Point

A4 must get as close to A3 as possible in order to receive the short 'lay off' pass.

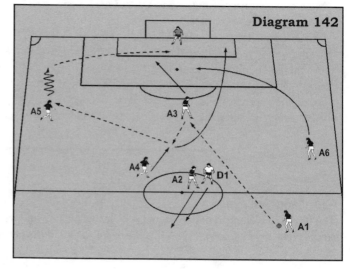

Diagram 142

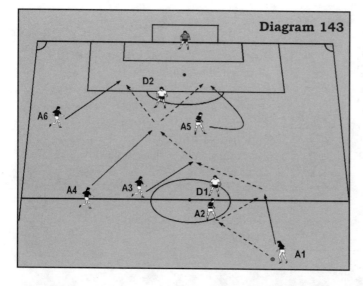

Diagram 143

Combination Four

Player A2 moves inside and toward the passer A1 taking defender D1 with him as in the previous combinations.
A1 plays to A2 and gets a one-touch return pass, then passes to A3 who has made a run to receive the ball.
A3 receives the ball with an open body position and passes to A4 who has made a run from his own half.
Player A4 then has the option of passing to either A5 or A6 who have made runs to receive the ball.

Coaching Points

- Timing of all runs is important
- A3 must have an 'open body position' to allow him to switch play to the opposite flank

Lira Lulea BK - Sweden

Combination Five

As in the previous combinations, A2 moves inside and toward the passer bringing his defender, D1 with him.

Player A1 passes to A2 who plays a one-touch pass to A3.

A3 times his run so he can receive a one-touch pass.

A3 then plays the ball wide to A4 who dribbles and crosses for A3, A5 and A6.

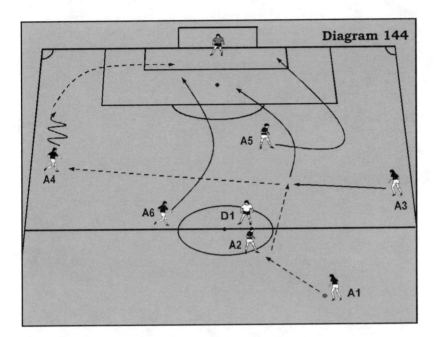

Coaching Points

• The timing of runs is extremely important
• The combinations must be practiced at game speed
• One touch finish if possible

AFC Manawatu - New Zealand

Contributed by Richard Hudson, head coach of the New Zealand First Division team, AFC Manawatu. This article is a technical/tactical training session focusing on "Third Man Running".

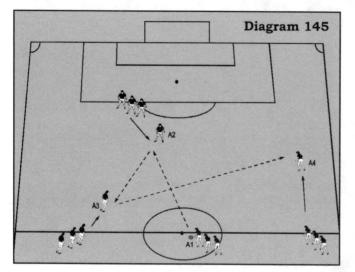

Half-Field Shadow Play

Organize the players in groups in a half-field as shown in diagram 145. This exercise helps the players become familiar with passing combinations designed to get the ball to the "third man". Player A1 passes long to incoming A2. A2 passes to the supporting player A3 who passes to the opposite flank for running A4.

Coaching Points
- Timing of runs
- Quality and weight of the passes
- Communication

Variation

If player A3 isn't able to play the long pass to A4 on the opposite flank, he can pass to A1 who can then pass to A4.

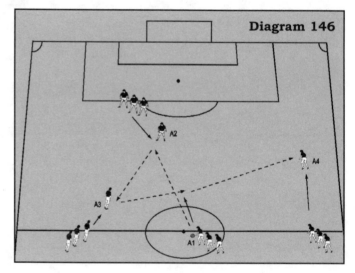

8 v 4 Pattern Play

Keep possession of the ball until an opportunity arises to pass the ball into a striker's feet. The striker passes to a supporting central midfielder who then passes to the opposite flank. Condition the play to two or three-touch. The deepest defender can play in a "safe zone" without being challenged. If the white team wins possession they attempt to keep the ball for as long as possible.

Coaching Points
- Strikers - play tight as a pair
- Central Midfielders - be a link between the defenders, strikers and wingers

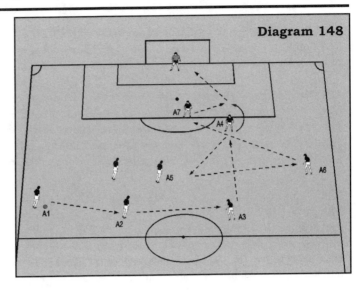

Diagram 148

Pattern Play

This combination includes passing wide to the third man running and includes the strikers working together by performing an "over". Player A1 passes to A2. A2 passes to A3. A3 passes to the "showing" striker, A4. A4 passes to the supporting midfielder, A5. A5 passes wide to A6. A6 plays an early pass to the feet of the striker, A4. The other striker, A7 shouts "over". This is the signal for A4 to let the ball run by him to A7. A4 spins, receives the one-touch pass from A7 and shoots.

Channel Game

Mark a half-field with wide channels as shown in diagram 149. Organize two teams each with a goalkeeper, two defenders, three midfielders and two strikers. Have a player in each channel who plays for the team in possession. Start off by playing shadow play going through the combinations practiced in the earlier exercises. Then play with a two or three-

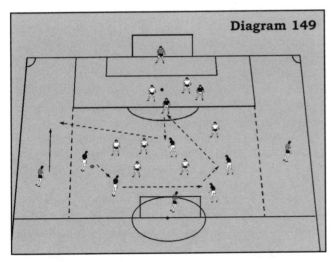

Diagram 149

touch restriction. Also, the strikers must play with their back to their own goal, are not allowed to turn with the ball and are limited to two touches.

Coaching Points
- The strikers must show for the ball
- The deep midfielders must support the strikers when they have the ball
- Timing of the runs to receive the ball from the wide players
- Quality of the pass to the wide player and the cross from the wide player
- Inventiveness of the finishing

Attack v Defense

Mark the field into zones as shown in diagram 150. The dark team attacks, the white team defends. Only players from the attacking team are allowed into the wide zones. Play 3 v 3 in the midfield zone and 2 v 2 in the attacking zone. This game is used to try the various combinations practiced earlier in a game-like situation.

Coaching Points
- All previous coaching points
- Keep possession but don't overplay - get the ball wide early and often

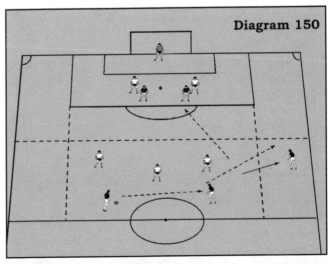

Diagram 150

Contributed by Mike Saif, editor and publisher of WORLD CLASS COACHING magazine. Mike participated in his first coaching course in his home country of England 20 years ago when he was just 19 years old. After arriving in the U.S. in 1991 Mike attended and passed the USSF "B" Licence in 1993 and the USSF "A" Licence in 1994.

Mike formed the 87 Dynamos Girls Team at the U10 age group although he had coached a number of the players in various other teams and clinics since they were 7 and 8 years old. Over the years the Dynamos have won a National Indoor Championship, three consecutive State Championships and a Region Two Championship before winning the 2001 USYSA/Snickers U14G National Championship. In this article, Mike explains what kind of schedule the team followed during their National Championship season and shares a typical training session.

Shadow Play

I often spend 10 - 15 minutes on shadow play going through various combinations. Toward the end of the spring season we worked on playing the ball into the forwards' feet and playing from there. I learned many of these combinations watching a session by Dick Bate, the coach of the England U16 National Team. After demonstrating a few combinations of what I was looking for at walking speed, the players would then perform them at game speed. I would then add a few defenders to make the game more realistic and ask the players to use any of the combinations or others that might seem appropriate.

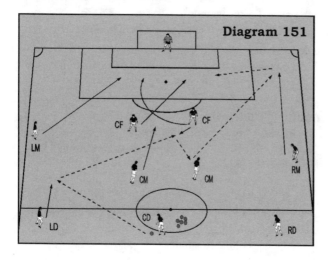

Shadow Play

In this combination the ball is passed from the center defender to the left defender.
The left defender passes to the center forward.
The center forward passes to the center midfielder.
The center midfielder switches the ball wide to the running right midfielder who crosses into the penalty area.
The left midfielder, both forwards and both center midfielders make timed runs toward the penalty area.

Shadow Play

In this combination the ball is passed from the right defender to the center midfielder.
The center midfielder passes to the center forward.
The center forward passes to the center midfielder.
The center midfielder switches the ball wide to the running left midfielder who crosses into the penalty area.
The right midfielder, both forwards and both center midfielders make timed runs toward the penalty area.

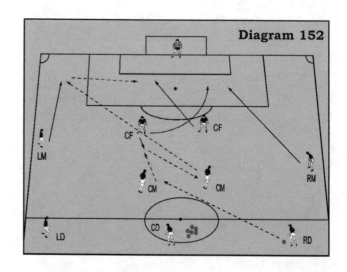

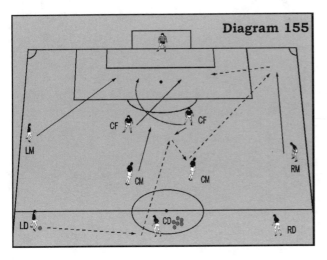

Diagram 155

Shadow Play

In this combination the ball is passed from the left defender to the center defender.

The center defender passes to the center forward.

The center forward passes to the center midfielder.

The center midfielder passes the ball wide to the running right midfielder who crosses into the penalty area.

The left midfielder, both forwards and both center midfielders make timed runs toward the penalty area.

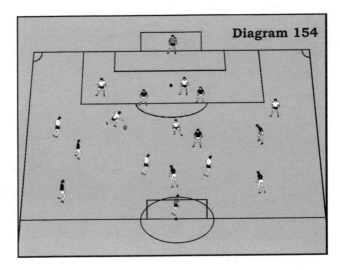

Diagram 154

Half-Field Game

Practice usually ends with a game played on a half-field. I will start the game with some conditions. For instance, in this game the players are only allowed to score a goal once the ball has been played into the forwards' feet (as we practiced with the shadow play). I rarely stop the game to get across any coaching points. However, I am constantly looking for, and encouraging the players to focus on what we have worked on earlier in the practice. In particular, I am always focusing on quality passing and receiving.

OTHER BOOKS IN THIS SERIES

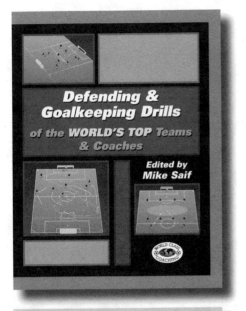

Defending and Goalkeeping Drills of the World's Top Teams and Coaches includes training sessions and drills from **Sao Paulo of Brazil, Italy U15 National Team, Tony DiCicco, Liverpool F.C., Lira Lulea BK of Sweden, Leeds United** plus **New England Revolution of the MLS** and other top teams and coaches from around the world.

Over 20 training sessions are included, each with detailed explanations accompanied with easy-to-read diagrams.

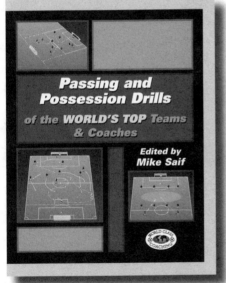

Passing and Possession Drills of the World's Top Teams and Coaches includes training sessions and drills from **Manchester United, Juventus F.C. and Venice of Serie "A", Ajax F.C., Lausanne of Switzerland, Liverpool Academy** plus many of the MLS Teams and other top teams and coaches from around the world.

Twenty-nine training sessions are included, each with detailed explanations accompanied with easy-to-read diagrams.

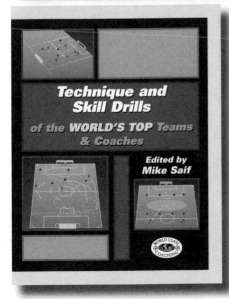

Technique and Skill Drills of the World's Top Teams and Coaches includes training sessions and drills from **PSV Eindhoven, U.S. Women's World Cup Team, Ajax F.C., Liverpool F.C., Leeds United, FK Teplice** plus many of the MLS Teams and other top teams and coaches from around the world.

Twenty-nine training sessions are included, each with detailed explanations accompanied with easy-to-read diagrams.

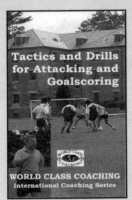
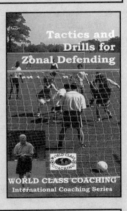

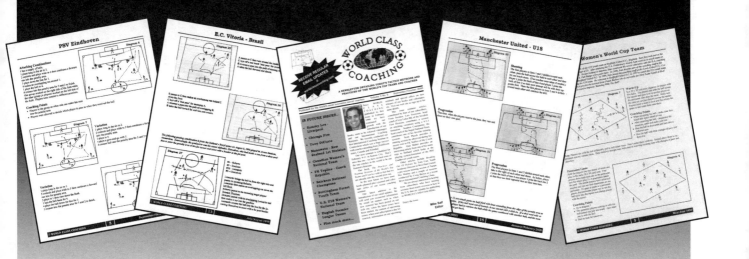